Powers of Criminal Courts Act 1973

CHAPTER 62

ARRANGEMENT OF SECTIONS

PART I

POWERS OF COURTS TO DEAL WITH OFFENDERS

Preliminary

Probation and discharge

Community service orders

Imprisonment, Borstal training and detention: general provisions

Supplemental

PART II

ADMINISTRATIVE AND SUPPLEMENTAL PROVISIONS

Rehabilitation of offenders and arrangements for persons on bail

Expenses and grants

Miscellaneous and supplemental

SCHEDULES:

Powers of Criminal Courts Act 1973

1973 CHAPTER 62

An Act to consolidate certain enactments relating to the powers of courts to deal with offenders and defaulters, to the treatment of offenders and to arrangements for persons on bail. [25th October 1973]

BE IT ENACTED by the Queen's most Excellent Majesty, by and with the advice and consent of the Lords Spiritual and Temporal, and Commons, in this present Parliament assembled, and by the authority of the same, as follows:—

PART I

POWERS OF COURTS TO DEAL WITH OFFENDERS

Preliminary

Deferment of sentence.

1.—(1) Subject to the provisions of this section, the Crown Court or a magistrates' court may defer passing sentence on an offender for the purpose of enabling the court to have regard, in determining his sentence, to his conduct after conviction (including, where appropriate, the making by him of reparation for his offence) or to any change in his circumstances.

(2) Any deferment under this section shall be until such date as may be specified by the court, not being more than six months after the date of the conviction; and where the passing of sentence has been deferred under this section it shall not be further deferred thereunder.

(3) The power conferred by this section shall be exercisable only if the offender consents and the court is satisfied, having regard to the nature of the offence and the character and circumstances of the offender, that it would be in the interests of justice to exercise the power.

PART I

(4) A court which under this section has deferred passing sentence on an offender may pass sentence on him before the expiration of the period of deferment if during that period he is convicted in Great Britain of any offence.

(5) Where a court which under this section has deferred passing sentence on an offender proposes to sentence him, whether on the date originally specified by the court or by virtue of subsection (4) above before that date, it may issue a summons requiring him to appear before the court, or may issue a warrant for his arrest.

1952 c. 55.

(6) Notwithstanding section 14(4) of the Magistrates' Courts Act 1952 (adjournment of trial), a magistrates' court shall not be obliged to remand an offender in whose case it defers the passing of sentence under this section.

(7) Nothing in this section shall affect the power of the Crown Court to bind over an offender to come up for judgment when called upon or the power of any court to defer passing sentence for any purpose for which it may lawfully do so apart from this section.

Probation and discharge

Probation.

2.—(1) Where a court by or before which a person of or over seventeen years of age is convicted of an offence (not being an offence the sentence for which is fixed by law) is of opinion that having regard to the circumstances, including the nature of the offence and the character of the offender, it is expedient to do so, the court may, instead of sentencing him, make a probation order, that is to say, an order requiring him to be under the supervision of a probation officer for a period to be specified in the order of not less than one year nor more than three years.

For the purposes of this subsection the age of a person shall be deemed to be that which it appears to the court to be after considering any available evidence.

(2) A probation order shall name the petty sessions area in which the offender resides or will reside; and the offender shall (subject to the provisions of Schedule 1 to this Act relating to probationers who change their residence) be required to be under the supervision of a probation officer appointed for or assigned to that area.

In this Act "supervising court" means, in relation to a probation order, a magistrates' court acting for the petty sessions area for the time being named in the order.

(3) Subject to the provisions of subsection (4) below and sections 3 and 4 of this Act a probation order may in addition

require the offender to comply during the whole or any part of the probation period with such requirements as the court, having regard to the circumstances of the case, considers necessary for securing the good conduct of the offender or for preventing a repetition by him of the same offence or the commission of other offences. PART I

(4) Without prejudice to the power of the court under section 35 of this Act to make a compensation order, the payment of sums by way of damages for injury or compensation for loss shall not be included among the requirements of a probation order.

(5) Without prejudice to the generality of subsection (3) above, a probation order may include requirements relating to the residence of the offender, but—

(*a*) before making an order containing any such requirements, the court shall consider the home surroundings of the offender; and

(*b*) where the order requires the offender to reside in an approved probation hostel, an approved probation home or any other institution, the name of the institution and the period for which he is so required to reside shall be specified in the order, and that period shall not extend beyond twelve months from the date of the order.

(6) Before making a probation order, the court shall explain to the offender in ordinary language the effect of the order (including any additional requirements proposed to be inserted therein under subsection (3) or (5) above or under section 3 or 4 of this Act) and that if he fails to comply with it or commits another offence he will be liable to be sentenced for the original offence; and the court shall not make the order unless he expresses his willingness to comply with its requirements.

(7) The court by which a probation order is made shall forthwith give copies of the order to a probation officer assigned to the court, and he shall give a copy to the offender, to the probation officer responsible for the supervision of the offender and to the person in charge of any institution in which the probationer is required by the order to reside; and the court shall, except where it is itself the supervising court, send to the clerk to the justices for the petty sessions area named in the order a copy of the order, together with such documents and information relating to the case as it considers likely to be of assistance to the supervising court.

PART I

(8) Where a probation order requires the offender to reside in any institution, not being—

(*a*) an approved probation hostel or approved probation home; or

(*b*) an institution in which he is required to reside for the purposes of any such treatment as is mentioned in section 3(2)(*a*) of this Act;

the court shall forthwith give notice of the terms of the order to the Secretary of State.

Probation orders requiring treatment for mental condition.
1959 c. 72.

3.—(1) Where the court is satisfied, on the evidence of a duly qualified medical practitioner approved for the purposes of section 28 of the Mental Health Act 1959, that the mental condition of an offender is such as requires and may be susceptible to treatment but is not such as to warrant his detention in pursuance of a hospital order under Part V of that Act, the court may, if it makes a probation order, include in it a requirement that the offender shall submit, during the whole of the probation period or during such part of that period as may be specified in the order, to treatment by or under the direction of a duly qualified medical practitioner with a view to the improvement of the offender's mental condition.

(2) The treatment required by any such order shall be such one of the following kinds of treatment as may be specified in the order, that is to say—

(*a*) treatment as a resident patient in a hospital or mental nursing home within the meaning of the Mental Health Act 1959, not being a special hospital within the meaning of that Act;

(*b*) treatment as a non-resident patient at such institution or place as may be specified in the order; or

(*c*) treatment by or under the direction of such duly qualified medical practitioner as may be specified in the order;

but the nature of the treatment shall not be specified in the order except as mentioned in paragraph (*a*), (*b*) or (*c*) above.

(3) A court shall not by virtue of this section include in a probation order a requirement that an offender shall submit to treatment for his mental condition unless it is satisfied that arrangements have been made for the treatment intended to be specified in the order (including arrangements for the reception of the offender where he is to be required to submit to treatment as a resident patient).

(4) While the probationer is under treatment as a resident patient in pursuance of a requirement of the probation order, the

probation officer responsible for his supervision shall carry out the supervision to such extent only as may be necessary for the purpose of the discharge or amendment of the order. **PART I**

(5) Where the medical practitioner by whom or under whose direction a probationer is being treated for his mental condition in pursuance of a probation order is of opinion that part of the treatment can be better or more conveniently given in or at an institution or place not specified in the order, being an institution or place in or at which the treatment of the probationer will be given by or under the direction of a duly qualified medical practitioner, he may, with the consent of the probationer, make arrangements for him to be treated accordingly; and the arrangements may provide for the probationer to receive part of his treatment as a resident patient in an institution or place notwithstanding that the institution or place is not one which could have been specified for that purpose in the probation order.

(6) Where any such arrangements as are mentioned in subsection (5) above are made for the treatment of a probationer—

(*a*) the medical practitioner by whom the arrangements are made shall give notice in writing to the probation officer responsible for the supervision of the probationer, specifying the institution or place in or at which the treatment is to be carried out; and

(*b*) the treatment provided for by the arrangements shall be deemed to be treatment to which he is required to submit in pursuance of the probation order.

(7) Subsections (2) and (3) of section 62 of the Mental Health Act 1959 shall have effect with respect to proof for the purposes of subsection (1) above of an offender's mental condition as they have effect with respect to proof of an offender's mental condition for the purposes of section 60(1)(*a*) of that Act. **1959 c. 72.**

(8) The provisions of this section shall apply in relation to a probation order made or amended by virtue of section 10 of this Act only so far as indicated in subsection (3) of that section, and except as provided by this section or section 10 a court shall not include in a probation order a requirement that the probationer shall submit to treatment for his mental condition.

Probation orders requiring attendance at day training centre.

4.—(1) Where a court makes a probation order in the case of an offender it may, subject to the provisions of this section, include in the order a requirement that he shall during the probation period attend at a day training centre specified in the order.

PART I

(2) A court shall not include such a requirement in a probation order unless—

(*a*) it has been notified by the Secretary of State that a day training centre exists for persons of the offender's class or description who reside in the petty sessions area in which he resides or will reside; and

(*b*) it is satisfied that arrangements can be made for his attendance at that centre;

and no such requirement shall be included in a probation order which includes a requirement under section 3 of this Act with respect to treatment of the probationer for his mental condition.

(3) A requirement included in a probation order by virtue of this section shall operate to require the probationer—

(*a*) in accordance with instructions given by the probation officer responsible for his supervision, to attend on not more than sixty days at the centre specified in the order;

(*b*) while attending there to comply with instructions given by, or under the authority of, the person in charge of the centre.

(4) References in this section to attendance at a day training centre include references to attendance elsewhere than at the centre for the purpose of receiving training in accordance with instructions given by, or under the authority of, the person in charge of the centre.

Discharge and amendment of probation orders.

5.—(1) The provisions of Schedule 1 to this Act shall have effect in relation to the discharge and amendment of probation orders.

(2) Where, under the following provisions of this Part of this Act, a probationer is sentenced for the offence for which he was placed on probation, the probation order shall cease to have effect.

Breach of requirement of probation order.

6.—(1) If at any time during the probation period it appears on information to a justice of the peace on whom jurisdiction is conferred by subsection (2) below that the probationer has failed to comply with any of the requirements of the order, the justice may issue a summons requiring the probationer to appear at the place and time specified therein, or may, if the information is in writing and on oath, issue a warrant for his arrest.

PART I

(2) The following justices shall have jurisdiction for the purposes of subsection (1) above, that is to say:—

(*a*) if the probation order was made by a magistrates' court, any justice acting for the petty sessions area for which that court or the supervising court acts;

(*b*) in any other case, any justice acting for the petty sessions area for which the supervising court acts;

and any summons or warrant issued under this section shall direct the probationer to appear or be brought before a magistrates' court acting for the petty sessions area for which the justice issuing the summons or warrant acts.

(3) If it is proved to the satisfaction of the magistrates' court before which a probationer appears or is brought under this section that the probationer has failed to comply with any of the requirements of the probation order, then, subject to the following provisions of this subsection, that court may deal with him in respect of the failure in any one of the following ways, that is to say:—

(*a*) it may impose on him a fine not exceeding £50;

(*b*) subject to subsection (10) below, it may make a community service order in respect of him;

(*c*) in a case to which section 19 of the Criminal Justice Act 1948 applies, it may make an order under that section requiring him to attend at an attendance centre; or 1948 c. 58.

(*d*) where the probation order was made by a magistrates' court, it may deal with him for the offence in respect of which the probation order was made, in any manner in which it could deal with him if it had just convicted him of that offence.

(4) Where the probation order was made by the Crown Court, and a magistrates' court has power to deal with the probationer under subsection (3)(*a*), (*b*) or (*c*) above in respect of a failure to comply with any of the requirements of the order, the magistrates' court may instead commit him to custody or release him on bail until he can be brought or appear before the Crown Court.

(5) A magistrates' court which deals with a probationer's case under subsection (4) above shall send to the Crown Court a certificate signed by a justice of the peace, certifying that the probationer has failed to comply with such of the requirements of the probation order as may be specified in the certificate, together with such other particulars of the case as may be desirable; and a certificate purporting to be so signed shall be admissible as evidence of the failure before the Crown Court.

PART I

(6) Where by virtue of subsection (4) above the probationer is brought or appears before the Crown Court, and it is proved to the satisfaction of the court that he has failed to comply with any of the requirements of the probation order, the court may deal with him in respect of the failure in any one of the following ways, that is to say:—

(*a*) it may impose on him a fine not exceeding £50;

(*b*) subject to subsection (10) below, it may make a community service order in respect of him; or

(*c*) it may deal with him for the offence in respect of which the probation order was made in any manner in which it could deal with him if he had just been convicted before the Crown Court of that offence.

(7) A probationer who is required by the probation order to submit to treatment for his mental condition shall not be treated for the purposes of this section as having failed to comply with that requirement on the ground only that he has refused to undergo any surgical, electrical or other treatment if, in the opinion of the court, his refusal was reasonable having regard to all the circumstances; and without prejudice to the provisions of section 8 of this Act, a probationer who is convicted of an offence committed during the probation period shall not on that account be liable to be dealt with under this section in respect of a failure to comply with any requirement of the probation order.

(8) Any exercise by a court of its powers under subsection (3)(*a*), (*b*) or (*c*) or (6)(*a*) or (*b*) above shall be without prejudice to the continuance of the probation order.

(9) A fine imposed under subsection (3)(*a*) above in respect of a failure to comply with the requirements of a probation order shall be deemed for the purposes of any enactment to be a sum adjudged to be paid by a conviction.

(10) Section 14(2) of this Act and, so far as applicable, the other provisions of this Act relating to community service orders shall have effect in relation to a community service order under this section as they have effect in relation to a community service order in respect of an offender, but as if the power conferred by sections 16 and 17 of this Act to deal with the offender for the offence in respect of which the community service order was made were a power to deal with the probationer for the failure to comply with the requirements of the probation order in respect of which the community service order was made.

PART I

Absolute and conditional discharge.

7.—(1) Where a court by or before which a person is convicted of an offence (not being an offence the sentence for which is fixed by law) is of opinion, having regard to the circumstances including the nature of the offence and the character of the offender, that it is inexpedient to inflict punishment and that a probation order is not appropriate, the court may make an order discharging him absolutely, or, if the court thinks fit, discharging him subject to the condition that he commits no offence during such period, not exceeding three years from the date of the order, as may be specified therein.

(2) An order discharging a person subject to such a condition is in this Act referred to as " an order for conditional discharge ", and the period specified in any such order (subject to section 8(1) of this Act) as " the period of conditional discharge ".

(3) Before making an order for conditional discharge the court shall explain to the offender in ordinary language that if he commits another offence during the period of conditional discharge he will be liable to be sentenced for the original offence.

(4) Where, under the following provisions of this Part of this Act, a person conditionally discharged under this section is sentenced for the offence in respect of which the order for conditional discharge was made, that order shall cease to have effect.

Commission of further offence by probationer or person conditionally discharged.

8.—(1) If it appears to the Crown Court, where that court has jurisdiction in accordance with subsection (2) below, or to a justice of the peace having jurisdiction in accordance with that subsection, that a person in whose case a probation order or an order for conditional discharge has been made has been convicted by a court in any part of Great Britain of an offence committed during the relevant period, and has been dealt with in respect of that offence, that court or justice may, subject to subsection (3) below, issue a summons requiring that person to appear at the place and time specified therein or a warrant for his arrest.

In this section " the relevant period " means, in relation to a probation order, the probation period, and in relation to an order for conditional discharge, the period of conditional discharge.

(2) Jurisdiction for the purposes of subsection (1) above may be exercised—

(*a*) if the probation order or order for conditional discharge was made by the Crown Court, by that court;

(*b*) if the order was made by a magistrates' court, by a justice acting for the petty sessions area for which that court acts;

PART I

(*c*) in the case of a probation order, by whatever court it was made, by a justice acting for the petty sessions area for which the supervising court acts.

(3) A justice of the peace shall not issue a summons under this section except on information and shall not issue a warrant under this section except on information in writing and on oath.

(4) Subject to subsection (5) below, a summons or warrant issued under this section shall direct the person to whom it relates to appear or to be brought before the court by which the probation order or the order for conditional discharge was made.

(5) In the case of a probation order made by a magistrates' court, a summons or warrant issued by a justice acting for the petty sessions area for which the supervising court acts may specify the supervising court instead of the court which made the order.

(6) If a person in whose case a probation order or an order for conditional discharge has been made by the Crown Court is convicted by a magistrates' court of an offence committed during the relevant period, the magistrates' court may commit him to custody or release him on bail until he he can be brought or appear before the Crown Court; and if it does so the magistrates' court shall send to the Crown Court a copy of the minute or memorandum of the conviction entered in the register, signed by the clerk of the court by whom the register is kept.

(7) Where it is proved to the satisfaction of the court by which a probation order or an order for conditional discharge was made, or to the satisfaction of that court or the supervising court in the case of a probation order made by a magistrates' court, that the person in whose case the order was made has been convicted of an offence committed during the relevant period, the court may deal with him, for the offence for which the order was made, in any manner in which it could deal with him if he had just been convicted by or before that court of that offence.

(8) If a person in whose case a probation order or an order for conditional discharge has been made by a magistrates' court is convicted before the Crown Court of an offence committed during the relevant period, or is dealt with by the Crown Court for any such offence in respect of which he was committed for sentence to the Crown Court, the Crown Court may deal with him, for the offence for which the order was made, in any manner in which the magistrates' court could deal with him if it had just convicted him of that offence.

Part I

(9) If a person in whose case a probation order or an order for conditional discharge has been made by a magistrates' court is convicted by another magistrates' court of any offence committed during the relevant period, that court may, with the consent of the court which made the order or, in the case of a probation order, with the consent of that court or of the supervising court, deal with him, for the offence for which the order was made, in any manner in which the court could deal with him if it had just convicted him of that offence.

Breach of conditional discharge by young offenders.

9.—(1) Where an order for conditional discharge has been made by a magistrates' court in the case of an offender under seventeen years of age in respect of an offence not being—

(*a*) a summary offence, or

(*b*) an offence which, in the case of an adult, could have been tried summarily with his consent under section 19 of the Magistrates' Courts Act 1952, 1952 c. 55.

any powers exercisable by that or any other court in respect of the offender after he has attained the age of seventeen years under subsection (7), (8) or (9) of section 8 of this Act shall be those which would be exercisable if that offence were such an offence as is mentioned in paragraph (*b*) above and had been tried summarily with his consent under section 19.

(2) For the purposes of this section the age of an offender at a particular time shall be deemed to be or to have been that which appears to the court after considering any available evidence to be or to have been his age at that time.

Probation orders relating to persons residing in Scotland.

10.—(1) Where the court by which a probation order is made under section 2 of this Act is satisfied that the offender resides or will reside in Scotland, subsection (2) of that section shall not apply to the order, but the order shall specify as the appropriate court for the purposes of this section a court of summary jurisdiction (which, in the case of an offender convicted on indictment, shall be the sheriff court) having jurisdiction in the place in Scotland in which the offender resides or will reside.

(2) Where a probation order has been made under section 2 of this Act and the supervising court is satisfied that the probationer proposes to reside or is residing in Scotland, the power of that court to amend the order under Schedule 1 to this Act shall include power to amend it by substituting for the provisions required by section 2(2) of this Act the provisions required by subsection (1) above; and the court may so amend the order without summoning the probationer and without his consent.

PART I

(3) A probation order made or amended by virtue of this section may include a requirement that the probationer shall submit to treatment for his mental condition, and—

(*a*) subsections (1), (3) and (7) of section 3 of this Act and subsection (2) of section 3 of the Criminal Justice (Scotland) Act 1949 (which makes equivalent provision to that made by section 3(2) of this Act) shall apply to the making of an order which includes any such requirement by virtue of this subsection as they apply to the making of an order which includes any such requirement by virtue of section 3 of this Act and of that Act respectively; and

1949 c. 94.

(*b*) subsections (4) to (6) of section 3 of that Act (functions of supervising officer and medical practitioner where such a requirement has been imposed) shall apply in relation to a probationer who is undergoing treatment in Scotland in pursuance of a requirement imposed by virtue of this subsection as they apply in relation to a probationer undergoing such treatment in pursuance of a requirement imposed by virtue of section 3 of that Act.

(4) Sections 5(1) and 6(1) and (2) of this Act shall not apply to any order made or amended by virtue of this section; but the provisions of the Criminal Justice (Scotland) Act 1949, except sections 5(2)(*b*) and 6 (sentencing the probationer for the offence for which the order was made), shall apply to the order as if it were a probation order made under section 2 of that Act and as if the court specified in the order as the appropriate court had been named as such under subsection (2) of that section.

(5) If in the case of a probation order made or amended by virtue of this section the appropriate court (as defined by the Criminal Justice (Scotland) Act 1949) is satisfied that the probationer has failed to comply with any requirement of the probation order, the court may, instead of dealing with him in any manner authorised by that Act, commit him to custody or release him on bail until he can be brought or appear before the court in England and Wales by which the probation order was made, and, if it so commits him or releases him on bail,—

(*a*) the court shall send to the court in England and Wales a certificate certifying that the probationer has failed to comply with such of the requirements of the probation order as may be specified in the certificate, together with such other particulars of the case as may be desirable;

PART I

(b) that court shall have the same powers as if the probationer had been brought or appeared before it in pursuance of a warrant or summons issued under section 6(1) of this Act;

and a certificate purporting to be signed by the clerk of the appropriate court shall be admissible as evidence of the failure before the court which made the probation order.

(6) In relation to a probation order made or amended by virtue of this section, the appropriate court (as defined by the Criminal Justice (Scotland) Act 1949) shall have jurisdiction for the purposes of section 8(1) of this Act. 1949 c. 94.

(7) The court by which a probation order is made or amended by virtue of this section shall send three copies of the order as made or amended to the clerk of the court specified in the order as the appropriate court, together with such documents and information relating to the case as it considers likely to be of assistance to that court; and section 2(7) of this Act, or paragraph 6 of Schedule 1 to this Act, as the case may be, shall not apply to any such order.

(8) Where a probation order which is amended by virtue of subsection (2) above is an order to which the provisions of this Act apply by virtue of section 7 of the Criminal Justice (Scotland) Act 1949 (probation orders under that Act relating to persons residing in England and Wales) then, notwithstanding anything in that section or this section, the order shall, as from the date of the amendment, have effect in all respects as if it were an order made under section 2 of that Act in the case of a person residing in Scotland, and as if the court specified as the appropriate court in the order as so amended had been named as such under subsection (2) of that section.

Substitution of conditional discharge for probation.

11.—(1) Where on an application made by the probationer or the probation officer it appears to the court having power to discharge a probation order that the order is no longer appropriate in the case of the probationer, the court may make, in substitution for the probation order, an order discharging him in respect of the original offence, subject to the condition that he commits no offence between the making of the order under this section and the expiration of the probation period.

(2) A person in respect of whom an order is made under this section shall so long as the condition mentioned in subsection (1) above continues in force be treated in all respects and in particular for the purposes of section 8 of this Act as if the original order made in his case had been an order for conditional discharge made by the court which made the original order and as if the period of conditional discharge were the same as the probation period.

PART I

(3) Where an application under this section is made by the probation officer, it may be heard in the absence of the probationer if the officer produces to the court a statement by him that he understands the effect of an order under this section and consents to the application being made.

(4) On the making of an order under this section the appropriate officer of the court shall forthwith give copies of the order to the probation officer, who shall give a copy to the person in respect of whom the order is made and to the person in charge of any institution in which that person was required by the probation order to reside.

Supplementary provision as to probation and discharge.

12.—(1) Any court may, on making a probation order or an order for conditional discharge under this Part of this Act, if it thinks it expedient for the purpose of the reformation of the offender, allow any person who consents to do so to give security for the good behaviour of the offender.

(2) For the purposes of this Act, except section 2(7) and paragraph 1 of Schedule 1, where a probation order or an order for conditional discharge has been made on appeal, the order shall be deemed to have been made by the court from which the appeal was brought.

(3) In proceedings before the Crown Court under the preceding provisions of this Act, any question whether a probationer has failed to comply with the requirements of the probation order, and any question whether any person in whose case a probation order or an order for conditional discharge has been made has been convicted of an offence committed during the probation period or, as the case may be, the period of conditional discharge, shall be determined by the court and not by the verdict of a jury.

(4) Nothing in section 2 or 7 of this Act shall be construed as taking away any power of the court, on making a probation order in respect of an offender or discharging an offender absolutely or conditionally, to order him to pay costs or compensation.

Effects of probation and discharge.

13.—(1) Subject to subsection (2) below, a conviction of an offence for which an order is made under this Part of this Act placing the offender on probation or discharging him absolutely or conditionally shall be deemed not to be a conviction for any purpose other than the purposes of the proceedings in which the order is made and of any subsequent proceedings which may be taken against the offender under the preceding provisions of this Act.

(2) Where the offender was of or over seventeen years of age at the time of his conviction of the offence in question and

is subsequently sentenced under this Part of this Act for that offence, subsection (1) above shall cease to apply to the conviction. PART I

(3) Without prejudice to the preceding provisions of this section, the conviction of an offender who is placed on probation or discharged absolutely or conditionally under this Part of this Act shall in any event be disregarded for the purposes of any enactment or instrument which imposes any disqualification or disability upon convicted persons, or authorises or requires the imposition of any such disqualification or disability.

(4) The preceding provisions of this section shall not affect—

(*a*) any right of any offender placed on probation or discharged absolutely or conditionally under this Part of this Act to appeal against his conviction, or to rely on it in bar of any subsequent proceedings for the same offence;

(*b*) the restoration of any property in consequence of the conviction of any such offender; or

(*c*) the operation, in relation to any such offender, of any enactment or instrument in force at the commencement of this Act which is expressed to extend to persons dealt with under section 1(1) of the Probation of Offenders Act 1907 as well as to convicted persons. 1907 c. 17.

(5) In this section " enactment " includes an enactment contained in a local Act and " instrument " means an instrument having effect by virtue of an Act.

Community service orders

Community service orders in respect of convicted persons.

14.—(1) Where a person of or over seventeen years of age is convicted of an offence punishable with imprisonment, the court by or before which he is convicted may, instead of dealing with him in any other way (but subject to subsection (2) below) make an order (in this Act referred to as " a community service order ") requiring him to perform unpaid work in accordance with the subsequent provisions of this Act for such number of hours (being in the aggregate not less than forty nor more than two hundred and forty) as may be specified in the order.

The reference in this subsection to an offence punishable with imprisonment shall be construed without regard to any prohibition or restriction imposed by or under any enactment on the imprisonment of young offenders.

PART I

(2) A court shall not make a community service order in respect of any offender unless the offender consents and the court—

(*a*) has been notified by the Secretary of State that arrangements exist for persons who reside in the petty sessions area in which the offender resides or will reside to perform work under such orders ; and

(*b*) is satisfied—

(i) after considering a report by a probation officer about the offender and his circumstances and, if the court thinks it necessary, hearing a probation officer, that the offender is a suitable person to perform work under such an order ; and

(ii) that provision can be made under the arrangements for him to do so.

(3) Where a court makes community service orders in respect of two or more offences of which the offender has been convicted by or before the court, the court may direct that the hours of work specified in any of those orders shall be concurrent with or additional to those specified in any other of those orders, but so that the total number of hours which are not concurrent shall not exceed the maximum in subsection (1) above.

(4) A community service order shall specify the petty sessions area in which the offender resides or will reside ; and the functions conferred by the subsequent provisions of this Act on the relevant officer shall be discharged by a probation officer appointed for or assigned to the area for the time being specified in the order (whether under this subsection or by virtue of section 17(5) of this Act), or by a person appointed for the purposes of those provisions by the probation and after-care committee for that area.

(5) Before making a community service order the court shall explain to the offender in ordinary language—

(*a*) the purpose and effect of the order (and in particular the requirements of the order as specified in section 15 of this Act) ;

(*b*) the consequences which may follow under section 16 if he fails to comply with any of those requirements ; and

(*c*) that the court has under section 17 the power to review the order on the application either of the offender or of a probation officer.

(6) The court by which a community service order is made shall forthwith give copies of the order to a probation officer assigned to the court and he shall give a copy to the offender and to the relevant officer ; and the court shall, except where it

PART I

is itself a magistrates' court acting for the petty sessions area specified in the order, send to the clerk to the justices for the petty sessions area specified in the order a copy of the order, together with such documents and information relating to the case as it considers likely to be of assistance to a court acting for that area in exercising its functions in relation to the order.

(7) The Secretary of State may by order direct that subsection (1) above shall be amended by substituting, for the maximum number of hours specified in that subsection as originally enacted or as previously amended under this subsection, such number of hours as may be specified in the order.

(8) Nothing in subsection (1) above shall be construed as preventing a court which makes a community service order in respect of any offence from making an order for costs against, or imposing any disqualification on, the offender or from making in respect of the offence an order under section 35, 39, 43 or 44 of this Act, or under section 28 of the Theft Act 1968. 1968 c. 60.

Obligations of person subject to community service order.

15.—(1) An offender in respect of whom a community service order is in force shall—

(*a*) report to the relevant officer and subsequently from time to time notify him of any change of address; and

(*b*) perform for the number of hours specified in the order such work at such times as he may be instructed by the relevant officer.

(2) Subject to section 17(1) of this Act, the work required to be performed under a community service order shall be performed during the period of twelve months beginning with the date of the order.

(3) The instructions given by the relevant officer under this section shall, so far as practicable, be such as to avoid any conflict with the offender's religious beliefs and any interference with the times, if any, at which he normally works or attends a school or other educational establishment.

Breach of requirements of community service order.

16.—(1) If at any time while a community service order is in force in respect of an offender it appears on information to a justice of the peace acting for the petty sessions area for the time being specified in the order that the offender has failed to comply with any of the requirements of section 15 of this Act (including any failure satisfactorily to perform the work which he has been instructed to do), the justice may issue a summons requiring the offender to appear at the place and time specified therein, or may, if the information is in writing and on oath, issue a warrant for his arrest.

PART I

(2) Any summons or warrant issued under this section shall direct the offender to appear or be brought before a magistrates' court acting for the petty sessions area for the time being specified in the community service order.

(3) If it is proved to the satisfaction of the magistrates' court before which an offender appears or is brought under this section that he has failed without reasonable excuse to comply with any of the requirements of section 15 the court may, without prejudice to the continuance of the order, impose on him a fine not exceeding £50 or may—

(*a*) if the community service order was made by a magistrates' court, revoke the order and deal with the offender, for the offence in respect of which the order was made, in any manner in which he could have been dealt with for that offence by the court which made the order if the order had not been made;

(*b*) if the order was made by the Crown Court, commit him to custody or release him on bail until he can be brought or appear before the Crown Court.

(4) A magistrates' court which deals with an offender's case under subsection (3)(*b*) above shall send to the Crown Court a certificate signed by a justice of the peace certifying that the offender has failed to comply with the requirements of section 15 in the respect specified in the certificate, together with such other particulars of the case as may be desirable; and a certificate purporting to be so signed shall be admissible as evidence of the failure before the Crown Court.

(5) Where by virtue of subsection (3)(*b*) above the offender is brought or appears before the Crown Court and it is proved to the satisfaction of the court that he has failed to comply with any of the requirements of section 15, that court may either—

(*a*) without prejudice to the continuance of the order, impose on him a fine not exceeding £50; or

(*b*) revoke the order and deal with him, for the offence in respect of which the order was made, in any manner in which he could have been dealt with for that offence by the court which made the order if the order had not been made.

(6) A person sentenced under subsection (3)(*a*) above for an offence may appeal to the Crown Court against the sentence.

(7) In proceedings before the Crown Court under this section any question whether the offender has failed to comply with the requirements of section 15 shall be determined by the court and not by the verdict of a jury.

(8) A fine imposed under this section shall be deemed for the purposes of any enactment to be a sum adjudged to be paid by a conviction.

Amendment and revocation of community service orders, and substitution of other sentences.

17.—(1) Where a community service order is in force in respect of any offender and, on the application of the offender or the relevant officer, it appears to a magistrates' court acting for the petty sessions area for the time being specified in the order that it would be in the interests of justice to do so having regard to circumstances which have arisen since the order was made, the court may extend, in relation to the order, the period of twelve months specified in section 15(2) of this Act.

(2) Where such an order is in force and on any such application it appears to a magistrates' court acting for the petty sessions area so specified that, having regard to such circumstances, it would be in the interests of justice that the order should be revoked or that the offender should be dealt with in some other manner for the offence in respect of which the order was made, the court may—

(*a*) if the order was made by a magistrates' court, revoke the order or revoke it and deal with the offender for that offence in any manner in which he could have been dealt with for that offence by the court which made the order if the order had not been made;

(*b*) if the order was made by the Crown Court, commit him to custody or release him on bail until he can be brought or appear before the Crown Court;

and where the court deals with his case under paragraph (*b*) above it shall send to the Crown Court such particulars of the case as may be desirable.

(3) Where by virtue of subsection (2)(*b*) above the offender is brought or appears before the Crown Court and it appears to the Crown Court to be in the interests of justice to do so, having regard to circumstances which have arisen since the order was made, the Crown Court may revoke the order or revoke the order and deal with the offender, for the offence in respect of which the order was made, in any manner in which he could have been dealt with for that offence by the court which made the order if the order had not been made.

(4) A person sentenced under subsection (2)(*a*) above for an offence may appeal to the Crown Court against the sentence.

(5) If a magistrates' court acting for the petty sessions area for the time being specified in a community service order is satisfied that the offender proposes to change, or has changed, his

residence from that petty sessions area to another petty sessions area and—

(*a*) the court has been notified that arrangements exist for persons who reside in that other area to perform work under community service orders; and

(*b*) it appears to the court that provision can be made under the arrangements for him to perform work under the order;

the court may, and on the application of the relevant officer shall, amend the order by substituting the other petty sessions area for the area specified in the order.

(6) Where a community service order is amended by a court under subsection (5) above the court shall send to the clerk to the justices for the new area specified in the order a copy of the order, together with such documents and information relating to the case as it considers likely to be of assistance to a court acting for that area in exercising its functions in relation to the order.

(7) Where a magistrates' court proposes to exercise its powers under subsection (1) or (2) above otherwise than on the application of the offender it shall summon him to appear before the court and, if he does not appear in answer to the summons, may issue a warrant for his arrest.

Imprisonment, Borstal training and detention: general provisions

General power of Crown Court to impose sentence of imprisonment on conviction on indictment.

18.—(1) Where a person is convicted on indictment of an offence against any enactment and is for that offence liable to be sentenced to imprisonment, but the sentence is not by any enactment either limited to a specified term or expressed to extend to imprisonment for life, the person so convicted shall be liable to imprisonment for not more than two years.

(2) A person convicted on indictment of an attempt to commit an offence for which a maximum term of imprisonment is provided by any enactment shall not be sentenced to imprisonment for a term longer than that to which he could be sentenced for the completed offence.

Restriction on imposing imprisonment on young offenders.

19.—(1) Neither the Crown Court nor a magistrates' court shall impose imprisonment on a person under seventeen years of age.

(2) No court shall impose imprisonment on a person under twenty-one years of age unless the court is of opinion that no other method of dealing with him is appropriate; and for the

purpose of determining whether any other method of dealing with any such person is appropriate the court shall obtain and consider information about the circumstances, and shall take into account any information before the court which is relevant to his character and his physical and mental condition.

PART I

(3) Where a magistrates' court imposes imprisonment on any such person as is mentioned in subsection (2) above, the court shall state the reason for its opinion that no other method of dealing with him is appropriate, and cause that reason to be specified in the warrant of commitment and to be entered in the register.

(4) In this section " impose imprisonment " means pass a sentence of imprisonment or commit to prison in default of payment of any sum of money, or for want of sufficient distress to satisfy any sum of money, or for failure to do or abstain from doing anything required to be done or left undone.

(5) For the purposes of this section and of section 20 of this Act the age of a person shall be deemed to be that which it appears to the court to be after considering any available evidence.

Restriction on imposing sentences of imprisonment on persons who have not previously served prison sentences.

20.—(1) No court shall pass a sentence of imprisonment on a person of or over twenty-one years of age on whom such a sentence has not previously been passed by a court in any part of the United Kingdom unless the court is of opinion that no other method of dealing with him is appropriate; and for the purpose of determining whether any other method of dealing with any such person is appropriate the court shall obtain and consider information about the circumstances, and shall take into account any information before the court which is relevant to his character and his physical and mental condition.

(2) Where a magistrates' court passes a sentence of imprisonment on any such person as is mentioned in subsection (1) above, the court shall state the reason for its opinion that no other method of dealing with him is appropriate, and cause that reason to be specified in the warrant of commitment and to be entered in the register.

(3) For the purposes of this section—

(*a*) a previous sentence of imprisonment which has been suspended and which has not taken effect under section 23 of this Act or under section 19 of the Treatment of Offenders Act (Northern Ireland) 1968 shall be disregarded; and

1968 c. 29 (N.I.).

PART I

(*b*) " sentence of imprisonment " does not include a committal or attachment for contempt of court.

(4) Subsection (1) above does not affect the power of a court to pass sentence on any person for an offence the sentence for which is fixed by law.

Restriction on imposing sentences of imprisonment, Borstal training or detention on persons not legally represented.

21.—(1) A magistrates' court on summary conviction or the Crown Court on committal for sentence or on conviction on indictment shall not pass a sentence of imprisonment, Borstal training or detention in a detention centre on a person who is not legally represented in that court and has not been previously sentenced to that punishment by a court in any part of the United Kingdom, unless either—

(*a*) he applied for legal aid and the application was refused on the ground that it did not appear his means were such that he required assistance ; or

(*b*) having been informed of his right to apply for legal aid and had the opportunity to do so, he refused or failed to apply.

(2) For the purposes of this section a person is to be treated as legally represented in a court if, but only if, he has the assistance of counsel or a solicitor to represent him in the proceedings in that court at some time after he is found guilty and before he is sentenced, and in subsection (1)(*a*) and (*b*) above " legal aid " means legal aid for the purposes of proceedings in that court, whether the whole proceedings or the proceedings on or in relation to sentence ; but in the case of a person committed to the Crown Court for sentence or trial, it is immaterial whether he applied for legal aid in the Crown Court to, or was informed of his right to apply by, that court or the court which committed him.

(3) For the purposes of this section—

(*a*) a previous sentence of imprisonment which has been suspended and which has not taken effect under section 23 of this Act or under section 19 of the Treatment of Offenders Act (Northern Ireland) 1968 shall be disregarded ;

1968 c. 29 (N.I.).

(*b*) " sentence of imprisonment " does not include a committal or attachment for contempt of court ; and

(*c*) " detention centre " means in relation to Northern Ireland young offenders centre.

Suspended sentences of imprisonment

Suspended sentences of imprisonment.

22.—(1) Subject to subsection (2) below, a court which passes a sentence of imprisonment for a term of not more than two years for an offence may order that the sentence shall not take effect unless, during a period specified in the order, being not less than one year or more than two years from the date of the order, the offender commits in Great Britain another offence punishable with imprisonment and thereafter a court having power to do so orders under section 23 of this Act that the original sentence shall take effect; and in this Part of this Act "operational period", in relation to a suspended sentence, means the period so specified. PART I

(2) A court shall not deal with an offender by means of a suspended sentence unless the case appears to the court to be one in which a sentence of imprisonment would have been appropriate in the absence of any power to suspend such a sentence by an order under subsection (1) above.

(3) A court which passes a suspended sentence on any person for an offence shall not make a probation order in his case in respect of another offence of which he is convicted by or before the court or for which he is dealt with by the court.

(4) On passing a suspended sentence the court shall explain to the offender in ordinary language his liability under section 23 of this Act if during the operational period he commits an offence punishable with imprisonment.

(5) Where a court has passed a suspended sentence on any person, and that person is subsequently sentenced to Borstal training, he shall cease to be liable to be dealt with in respect of the suspended sentence unless the subsequent sentence or any conviction or finding on which it was passed is quashed on appeal.

(6) Subject to any provision to the contrary contained in the Criminal Justice Act 1967, this Act or any enactment passed or instrument made under any enactment after 31st December 1967— 1967 c. 80.

(*a*) a suspended sentence which has not taken effect under section 23 of this Act shall be treated as a sentence of imprisonment for the purposes of all enactments and instruments made under enactments except any enactment or instrument which provides for disqualification for or loss of office, or forfeiture of pensions, of persons sentenced to imprisonment; and

(*b*) where a suspended sentence has taken effect under that section, the offender shall be treated for the purposes of the enactments and instruments excepted by paragraph (*a*) above as having been convicted on the ordinary date on which the period allowed for making an appeal against an order under that section expires or, if such an appeal is made, the date on which it is finally disposed of or abandoned or fails for non-prosecution.

PART I

Power of court on conviction of further offence to deal with suspended sentence.

23.—(1) Where an offender is convicted of an offence punishable with imprisonment committed during the operational period of a suspended sentence and either he is so convicted by or before a court having power under section 24 of this Act to deal with him in respect of the suspended sentence or he subsequently appears or is brought before such a court, then, unless the sentence has already taken effect, that court shall consider his case and deal with him by one of the following methods:—

(*a*) the court may order that the suspended sentence shall take effect with the original term unaltered;

(*b*) it may order that the sentence shall take effect with the substitution of a lesser term for the original term;

(*c*) it may by order vary the original order under section 22(1) of this Act by substituting for the period specified therein a period expiring not later than two years from the date of the variation; or

(*d*) it may make no order with respect to the suspended sentence;

and a court shall make an order under paragraph (*a*) of this subsection unless the court is of opinion that it would be unjust to do so in view of all the circumstances which have arisen since the suspended sentence was passed, including the facts of the subsequent offence, and where it is of that opinion the court shall state its reasons.

(2) Where a court orders that a suspended sentence shall take effect, with or without any variation of the original term, the court may order that that sentence shall take effect immediately or that the term thereof shall commence on the expiration of another term of imprisonment passed on the offender by that or another court.

(3) Where under subsection (1)(*a*) or (*b*) above a court orders that a suspended sentence shall take effect with a term of not more than six months and the court would have had power to sentence the offender to be detained in a detention centre for that term if it had convicted him of the original offence on the occasion of the order, the order may include a direction that he shall serve the sentence in a detention centre.

(4) Without prejudice to subsection (3) above, where under subsection (1)(*a*) or (*b*) above a court orders that a suspended sentence shall take effect with a term of less than three months, the court may include such a direction in the order if the offender is then liable to be detained in a detention centre by virtue of an order or warrant made or issued by that or another court.

PART I

(5) An order under subsection (1)(*a*) or (*b*) above which includes such a direction shall be treated for all purposes as an order under section 4 of the Criminal Justice Act 1961 (detention of offenders under twenty-one) for the detention of the offender in a detention centre, and subsection (2) above shall not apply in relation to any such order.

1961 c. 39.

(6) In proceedings for dealing with an offender in respect of a suspended sentence which take place before the Crown Court any question whether the offender has been convicted of an offence punishable with imprisonment committed during the operational period of the suspended sentence shall be determined by the court and not by the verdict of a jury.

(7) Where a court deals with an offender under this section in respect of a suspended sentence the appropriate officer of the court shall notify the appropriate officer of the court which passed the sentence of the method adopted.

(8) Where on consideration of the case of an offender a court makes no order with respect to a suspended sentence, the appropriate officer of the court shall record that fact.

(9) For the purposes of any enactment conferring rights of appeal in criminal cases any order made by a court with respect to a suspended sentence shall be treated as a sentence passed on the offender by that court for the offence for which the suspended sentence was passed.

Court by which suspended sentence may be dealt with.

24.—(1) An offender may be dealt with in respect of a suspended sentence by the Crown Court or, where the sentence was passed by a magistrates' court, by any magistrates' court before which he appears or is brought.

(2) Where an offender is convicted by a magistrates' court of an offence punishable with imprisonment and the court is satisfied that the offence was committed during the operational period of a suspended sentence passed by the Crown Court—

(*a*) the court may, if it thinks fit, commit him in custody or on bail to the Crown Court; and

(*b*) if it does not, shall give written notice of the conviction to the appropriate officer of the Crown Court.

(3) For the purposes of this section and of section 25 of this Act a suspended sentence passed on an offender on appeal shall be treated as having been passed by the court by which he was originally sentenced.

PART I

Procedure where court convicting of further offence does not deal with suspended sentence.

25.—(1) If it appears to the Crown Court, where that court has jurisdiction in accordance with subsection (2) below, or to a justice of the peace having jurisdiction in accordance with that subsection, that an offender has been convicted in Great Britain of an offence punishable with imprisonment committed during the operational period of a suspended sentence and that he has not been dealt with in respect of the suspended sentence, that court or justice may, subject to the following provisions of this section, issue a summons requiring the offender to appear at the place and time specified therein, or a warrant for his arrest.

(2) Jurisdiction for the purposes of subsection (1) above may be exercised—

(*a*) if the suspended sentence was passed by the Crown Court, by that court;

(*b*) if it was passed by a magistrates' court, by a justice acting for the area for which that court acted.

(3) Where an offender is convicted by a court in Scotland of an offence punishable with imprisonment and the court is informed that the offence was committed during the operational period of a suspended sentence passed in England or Wales, the court shall give written notice of the conviction to the appropriate officer of the court by which the suspended sentence was passed.

(4) Unless he is acting in consequence of a notice under subsection (3) above, a justice of the peace shall not issue a summons under this section except on information and shall not issue a warrant under this section except on information in writing and on oath.

(5) A summons or warrant issued under this section shall direct the offender to appear or to be brought before the court by which the suspended sentence was passed.

Suspended sentence supervision orders.

26.—(1) Where a court passes on an offender a suspended sentence for a term of more than six months for a single offence, the court may make a suspended sentence supervision order (in this Act referred to as " a supervision order ") placing the offender under the supervision of a supervising officer for a period specified in the order, being a period not exceeding the operational period of the suspended sentence.

(2) The Secretary of State may by order—

(*a*) direct that subsection (1) above be amended by substituting, for the number of months specified in the subsection as originally enacted or as previously amended under this paragraph, such other number (not more than six) as the order may specify; or

(b) make in that subsection the repeals necessary to enable a court to make a supervision order thereunder in the case of any suspended sentence, whatever the length of the term. PART I

(3) A supervision order shall specify the petty sessions area in which the offender resides or will reside; and the supervising officer shall be a probation officer appointed for or assigned to the area for the time being specified in the order (whether under this subsection or by virtue of subsection (6) below).

(4) An offender in respect of whom a supervision order is in force shall keep in touch with the supervising officer in accordance with such instructions as he may from time to time be given by that officer and shall notify him of any change of address.

(5) The court by which a supervision order is made shall forthwith give copies of the order to a probation officer assigned to the court, and he shall give a copy to the offender and the supervising officer; and the court shall, except where it is itself a magistrates' court acting for the petty sessions area specified in the order, send to the clerk to the justices for the petty sessions area specified in the order a copy of the order, together with such documents and information relating to the case as it considers likely to be of assistance to a court acting for that area in exercising its functions in relation to the order.

(6) If a magistrates' court acting for the petty sessions area for the time being specified in a supervision order is satisfied that the offender proposes to change, or has changed, his residence from that petty sessions area to another petty sessions area, the court may, and on the application of the supervising officer shall, amend the order by substituting the other petty sessions area for the area specified in the order.

(7) Where a supervision order is amended by a court under subsection (6) above the court shall send to the clerk to the justices for the new area specified in the order a copy of the order, together with such documents and information relating to the case as it considers likely to be of assistance to a court acting for that area in exercising its functions in relation to the order.

(8) A supervision order shall cease to have effect if before the end of the period specified in it—

(a) a court orders under section 23 of this Act that a suspended sentence passed in the proceedings in which the order was made shall have effect; or

(b) the order is discharged or replaced under the subsequent provisions of this section.

PART I

(9) A supervision order may be discharged, on the application of the supervising officer or the offender—

(*a*) if it was made by the Crown Court and includes a direction reserving the power of discharging it to that court, by the Crown Court;

(*b*) in any other case by a magistrates' court acting for the petty sessions area for the time being specified in the order.

(10) Where under section 23 of this Act a court deals with an offender in respect of a suspended sentence by varying the operational period of the sentence or by making no order with respect to the sentence, the court may make a supervision order in respect of the offender—

(*a*) in place of any such order made when the suspended sentence was passed; or

(*b*) if the court which passed the sentence could have made such an order but did not do so; or

(*c*) if that court could not then have made such an order but would have had power to do so if subsection (1) above had then had effect as it has effect at the time when the offender is dealt with under section 23.

(11) On making a supervision order the court shall in ordinary language explain its effect to the offender.

Breach of requirement of suspended sentence supervision order.

27.—(1) If at any time while a supervision order is in force in respect of an offender it appears on information to a justice of the peace acting for the petty sessions area for the time being specified in the order that the offender has failed to comply with any of the requirements of section 26(4) of this Act, the justice may issue a summons requiring the offender to appear at the place and time specified therein, or may, if the information is in writing and on oath, issue a warrant for his arrest.

(2) Any summons or warrant issued under this section shall direct the offender to appear or be brought before a magistrates' court acting for the petty sessions area for the time being specified in the supervision order.

(3) If it is proved to the satisfaction of the court before which an offender appears or is brought under this section that he has failed without reasonable cause to comply with any of the requirements of section 26(4) the court may, without prejudice to the continuance of the order, impose on him a fine not exceeding £50.

(4) A fine imposed under this section shall be deemed for the purposes of any enactment to be a sum adjudged to be paid by a conviction.

PART I

Powers relating to persistent offenders

Punishment of persistent offenders.

28.—(1) Where an offender is convicted on indictment of an offence punishable with imprisonment for a term of two years or more and the conditions specified in subsection (3) below are satisfied, then, if the court is satisfied, by reason of his previous conduct and of the likelihood of his committing further offences, that it is expedient to protect the public from him for a substantial time, the court may impose an extended term of imprisonment under this section.

(2) The extended term which may be imposed under this section for any offence may exceed the maximum term authorised for the offence apart from this section if the maximum so authorised is less than ten years, but shall not exceed ten years if the maximum so authorised is less than ten years or exceed five years if the maximum so authorised is less than five years.

(3) The conditions referred to in subsection (1) above are:—

(*a*) the offence was committed before the expiration of three years from a previous conviction of an offence punishable on indictment with imprisonment for a term of two years or more or from his final release from prison after serving a sentence of imprisonment, corrective training or preventive detention passed on such a conviction ; and

(*b*) the offender has been convicted on indictment on at least three previous occasions since he attained the age of twenty-one of offences punishable on indictment with imprisonment for a term of two years or more ; and

(*c*) the total length of the sentences of imprisonment, corrective training or preventive detention to which he was sentenced on those occasions was not less than five years and—

(i) on at least one of those occasions a sentence of preventive detention was passed on him ; or

(ii) on at least two of those occasions a sentence of imprisonment (other than a suspended sentence which has not taken effect) or of corrective training was so passed and of those sentences one was a sentence of imprisonment for a term of three years or more in respect of one offence or two were sentences of imprisonment each for a term of two years or more in respect of one offence.

(4) Where an extended term of imprisonment is imposed on an offender under this section, the court shall issue a certificate (hereafter in this Act referred to as "an extended sentence certificate") stating that the term was so imposed.

PART I

Supplementary provisions as to persistent offenders.

29.—(1) For the purposes of section 28(3)(*a*) of this Act a certificate purporting to be signed by the governor of a prison to the effect—

(*a*) that a prisoner was finally released from that prison on a date specified in the certificate after serving a sentence so specified ; or

(*b*) that a prisoner had not been finally released from that prison on a date so specified after serving a sentence so specified ;

shall be evidence of the matter so certified.

(2) For the purposes of section 28(3)(*b*) of this Act a person who has been convicted by a magistrates' court of an indictable offence and sentenced for that offence—

(*a*) by the Crown Court, or on appeal from the Crown Court, to imprisonment ; or

(*b*) by a court of quarter sessions, or on appeal from such a court, to imprisonment, corrective training or preventive detention ;

shall be treated as if he had been convicted of that offence on indictment.

(3) For the purpose of determining whether the conditions specified in section 28(3) of this Act are satisfied in relation to an offender no account shall be taken of any previous conviction or sentence unless notice has been given to the offender at least three days before the later sentence is passed on him that it is intended to prove the previous conviction or sentence to the court.

(4) For the purpose of subsection (3) above a certificate purporting to be signed by a constable or a prison officer that a copy of a notice annexed to the certificate was given to an offender shall be evidence that it was so given and of the contents of the notice.

(5) In this section and in section 28 of this Act " final release " includes a release on licence under section 60 or 61 of the Criminal Justice Act 1967, but does not include any temporary discharge.

1967 c. 80.

(6) A person sentenced at any time to corrective training or preventive detention in Scotland or Northern Ireland and transferred under section 26 of the Criminal Justice Act 1961 to England and Wales shall be treated for the purposes of detention, release, recall and otherwise as having been sentenced in England and Wales to a term of imprisonment of the same length as the term of his original sentence and, if he was originally sentenced to preventive detention, he shall also be so treated as if an extended sentence certificate had been issued in respect of him.

1961 c. 39.

PART I

(7) A person sentenced to an extended term of imprisonment under section 28 of this Act and transferred under section 26 of the Criminal Justice Act 1961 to Scotland or Northern Ireland shall, notwithstanding anything in section 26(4) (treatment of prisoners so transferred) be treated as if an extended sentence certificate had not been issued in respect of him.

1961 c. 39.

Crown Court fines, etc.

General power of Crown Court to fine offender convicted on indictment.

30.—(1) Where a person is convicted on indictment of any offence other than an offence for which the sentence is fixed by law, the court, if not precluded from sentencing the offender by its exercise of some other power (such as the power to make a probation order), may impose a fine in lieu of or in addition to dealing with him in any other way in which the court has power to deal with him, subject however to any enactment limiting the amount of the fine that may be imposed or requiring the offender to be dealt with in a particular way.

(2) A person convicted on indictment of an attempt to commit an offence for which a maximum fine is provided by any enactment shall not be sentenced to a fine larger than that to which he could be sentenced for the completed offence.

Powers, etc., of Crown Court in relation to fines and forfeited recognizances.

31.—(1) Subject to the provisions of this section, if the Crown Court imposes a fine on any person or forfeits his recognizance, the court may make an order—

(*a*) allowing time for the payment of the amount of the fine or the amount due under the recognizance;

(*b*) directing payment of that amount by instalments of such amounts and on such dates respectively as may be specified in the order;

(*c*) in the case of a recognizance, discharging the recognizance or reducing the amount due thereunder.

(2) Subject to the provisions of this section, if the Crown Court imposes a fine on any person or forfeits his recognizance, the court shall make an order fixing a term of imprisonment which that person is to undergo if any sum which he is liable to pay is not duly paid or recovered.

(3) A term of imprisonment fixed under subsection (2) above shall not exceed 12 months, and no person shall on the occasion when a fine is imposed on him or his recognizance is forfeited by the Crown Court be committed to prison in pursuance of an order under that subsection unless—

(*a*) in the case of an offence punishable with imprisonment, he appears to the court to have sufficient means to pay the sum forthwith;

PART I

(*b*) it appears to the court that he is unlikely to remain long enough at a place of abode in the United Kingdom to enable payment of the sum to be enforced by other methods ; or

(*c*) on the occasion when the order is made the court sentences him to immediate imprisonment or detention in a detention centre for that or another offence, or sentences him as aforesaid for an offence in addition to forfeiting his recognizance, or he is already serving a term of imprisonment or detention in a detention centre.

(4) Where any person liable for the payment of a fine or a sum due under a recognizance to which this section applies is sentenced by the court to, or is serving or otherwise liable to serve, a term of imprisonment, the court may order that any term of imprisonment fixed under subsection (2) above shall not begin to run until after the end of the first-mentioned term of imprisonment.

(5) The power conferred by this section to discharge a recognizance or reduce the amount due thereunder shall be in addition to the powers conferred by any other Act relating to the discharge, cancellation, mitigation or reduction of recognizances or sums forfeited thereunder.

(6) Subject to subsection (7) below, the powers conferred by this section shall not be taken as restricted by any enactment about committal by a magistrates' court to the Crown Court which authorises the Crown Court to deal with an offender in any way in which the magistrates' court might have dealt with him.

(7) Any term fixed under subsection (2) above as respects a fine imposed in pursuance of such an enactment, that is to say a fine which the magistrates' court could have imposed, shall not exceed the period applicable to that fine (if imposed by the magistrates' court) under Schedule 3 to the Magistrates' Courts Act 1952 or section 285 of the Customs and Excise Act 1952.

1952 c. 55.
1952 c. 44.

(8) This section shall not apply to a fine imposed by the Crown Court on appeal against a decision of a magistrates' court, but subsections (2) and (3) above shall apply in relation to a fine imposed or recognizance forfeited by the criminal division of the Court of Appeal, or by the House of Lords on appeal from that division, as they apply in relation to a fine imposed or recognizance forfeited by the Crown Court, and references in those subsections to the Crown Court shall be construed accordingly.

Part I

Enforcement, etc., of fines imposed and recognizances forfeited by Crown Court.

32.—(1) Subject to the provisions of subsection (4) below, a fine imposed or a recognizance forfeited by the Crown Court after 31st December 1967 shall be treated for the purposes of collection, enforcement and remission of the fine or other sum as having been imposed or forfeited—

(*a*) by a magistrates' court specified in an order made by the Crown Court; or

(*b*) if no such order is made, by the magistrates' court by which the offender was committed to the Crown Court to be tried or dealt with;

and in the case of a fine as having been so imposed on conviction by the magistrates' court in question.

(2) The term of imprisonment specified in any warrant of commitment issued by a magistrates' court on a default in the payment of a fine imposed, or sum due under a recognizance forfeited, by the Crown Court as the term which the offender is liable to serve shall be the term fixed by the latter court under section 31(2) of this Act or, if that term has been reduced under section 67(2) of the Magistrates' Courts Act 1952 (part payment) or section 44(10) of the Criminal Justice Act 1967 (remission) that term as so reduced, notwithstanding that that term exceeds the period applicable to the case under Schedule 3 to the Magistrates' Courts Act 1952 or section 285 of the Customs and Excise Act 1952 (maximum periods of imprisonment in default of payment of fines, etc.).

1952 c. 55.
1967 c. 80.
1952 c. 44.

(3) The preceding provisions of this section shall apply in relation to a fine imposed or recognizance forfeited by the criminal division of the Court of Appeal, or by the House of Lords on appeal from that division, as they apply in relation to a fine imposed or recognizance forfeited by the Crown Court, and references in those provisions to the Crown Court shall be construed accordingly.

(4) A magistrates' court shall not under section 44(10) of the Criminal Justice Act 1967 or section 96 of the Magistrates' Courts Act 1952, as applied by subsection (1) above, remit the whole or any part of a fine imposed or a sum due under a recognizance forfeited by the Crown Court without the consent of that court, and section 44(10) shall have effect accordingly.

(5) A fine imposed or a recognizance forfeited by the criminal division of the Court of Appeal on appeal from the Crown Court or by the House of Lords on appeal from that division shall be treated for the purposes of collection, enforcement and remission of the fine or other sum as having been imposed or forfeited by the Crown Court.

PART I

1949 c. 101.

(6) Any fine or other sum the payment of which is enforceable by a magistrates' court by virtue of this section shall be treated for the purposes of the Justices of the Peace Act 1949 and, in particular, section 27 thereof (application of fines imposed by magistrates' courts) as having been imposed by a magistrates' court, or as being due under a recognizance forfeited by such a court.

Transfer to Scotland of fines imposed and recognizances forfeited by Crown Court.
1952 c. 55.

33. The power of a magistrates' court to make a transfer of fine order under section 72A of the Magistrates' Courts Act 1952 (transfer of fine orders to Scotland) shall be exercisable in relation to a fine imposed on any person or a sum due from any person under a recognizance forfeited by the Crown Court the payment of which is enforceable by the magistrates' court, notwithstanding that the Crown Court has in pursuance of section 31(2) of this Act fixed a term of imprisonment which that person is to undergo if the fine or other sum is not duly paid or recovered.

Power of Crown Court to allow time for payment, or payment by instalments, of costs and compensation.
1970 c. 31.

34. Where the Crown Court makes any such order as is mentioned in Part I of Schedule 9 to the Administration of Justice Act 1970 (orders against accused for the payment of costs or compensation), the court may—

(*a*) allow time for the payment of the sum due under the order ;

(*b*) direct payment of that sum by instalments of such amounts and on such dates respectively as the court may specify.

Compensation orders

Compensation orders against convicted persons.

35.—(1) Subject to the provisions of this Part of this Act, a court by or before which a person is convicted of an offence, in addition to dealing with him in any other way, may, on application or otherwise, make an order (in this Act referred to as " a compensation order ") requiring him to pay compensation for any personal injury, loss or damage resulting from that offence or any other offence which is taken into consideration by the court in determining sentence.

1968 c. 60.

(2) In the case of an offence under the Theft Act 1968, where the property in question is recovered, any damage to the property occurring while it was out of the owner's possession shall be treated for the purposes of subsection (1) above as having resulted from the offence, however and by whomsoever the damage was caused.

(3) No compensation order shall be made in respect of loss suffered by the dependants of a person in consequence of his death, and no such order shall be made in respect of injury,

loss or damage due to an accident arising out of the presence of a motor vehicle on a road, except such damage as is treated by subsection (2) above as resulting from an offence under the Theft Act 1968. PART I 1968 c. 60.

(4) In determining whether to make a compensation order against any person, and in determining the amount to be paid by any person under such an order, the court shall have regard to his means so far as they appear or are known to the court.

(5) The compensation to be paid under a compensation order made by a magistrates' court in respect of any offence of which the court has convicted the offender shall not exceed £400; and the compensation or total compensation to be paid under a compensation order or compensation orders made by a magistrates' court in respect of any offence or offences taken into consideration in determining sentence shall not exceed the difference (if any) between the amount or total amount which under the preceding provisions of this subsection is the maximum for the offence or offences of which the offender has been convicted and the amount or total amounts (if any) which are in fact ordered to be paid in respect of that offence or those offences.

Appeals in the case of compensation orders. 1968 c. 19.

36.—(1) A compensation order made on conviction on indictment shall be treated for the purposes of sections 30 and 42(1) and (2) of the Criminal Appeal Act 1968 (effect of appeals on orders for the restitution of property) as an order for the restitution of property; and where by reason of the quashing by the Court of Appeal of a person's conviction any such order does not take effect, and on an appeal to the House of Lords the conviction is restored by that House, the House may make any compensation order which could be made on his conviction by the court which convicted him.

(2) A compensation order made by a magistrates' court shall be suspended—

(*a*) in any case until the expiration of the period for the time being prescribed by law for the giving of notice of appeal against a decision of a magistrates' court;

(*b*) where notice of appeal is given within the period so prescribed, until the determination of the appeal.

(3) Where a compensation order has been made against any person in respect of an offence taken into consideration in determining his sentence—

(*a*) the order shall cease to have effect if he successfully appeals against his conviction of the offence or, if more than one, all the offences, of which he was convicted in the proceedings in which the order was made;

PART I

(*b*) he may appeal against the order as if it were part of the sentence imposed in respect of the offence or, if more than one, any of the offences, of which he was so convicted.

Review of compensation orders.

1970 c. 31.

37. At any time before a compensation order has been complied with or fully complied with, the magistrates' court for the time being having functions in relation to the enforcement of the order (by virtue of section 41(1) of the Administration of Justice Act 1970) may, on the application of the person against whom it was made, discharge the order, or reduce the amount which remains to be paid, if it appears to the court—

(*a*) that the injury, loss or damage in respect of which the order was made has been held in civil proceedings to be less than it was taken to be for the purposes of the order; or

(*b*) in the case of an order in respect of the loss of any property, that the property has been recovered by the person in whose favour the order was made.

Effect of compensation order on subsequent award of damages in civil proceedings.

38.—(1) This section shall have effect where a compensation order has been made in favour of any person in respect of any injury, loss or damage and a claim by him in civil proceedings for damages in respect thereof subsequently falls to be determined.

(2) The damages in the civil proceedings shall be assessed without regard to the order; but where the whole or part of the amount awarded by the order has been paid, the damages awarded in the civil proceedings shall not exceed the amount (if any) by which, as so assessed, they exceed the amount paid under the order.

(3) Where the whole or part of the amount awarded by the order remains unpaid and the court awards damages in the civil proceedings, then, unless the person against whom the order was made has ceased to be liable to pay the amount unpaid (whether in consequence of an appeal, of his imprisonment for default or otherwise), the court shall direct that the judgment—

(*a*) if it is for an amount not exceeding the amount unpaid under the order, shall not be enforced; or

(*b*) if it is for an amount exceeding the amount unpaid under the order, shall not be enforced as to a corresponding amount;

without the leave of the court.

PART I

Criminal bankruptcy orders

Criminal bankruptcy orders against convicted persons.

39.—(1) Where a person is convicted of an offence before the Crown Court and it appears to the court that—

(*a*) as a result of the offence, or of that offence taken together with any other relevant offence or offences, loss or damage (not attributable to personal injury) has been suffered by one or more persons whose identity is known to the court; and

(*b*) the amount, or aggregate amount, of the loss or damage exceeds £15,000;

the court may, in addition to dealing with the offender in any other way (but not if it makes a compensation order against him), make a criminal bankruptcy order against him in respect of the offence or, as the case may be, that offence and the other relevant offence or offences.

(2) In subsection (1) above " other relevant offence or offences " means an offence or offences of which the person in question is convicted in the same proceedings or which the court takes into consideration in determining his sentence.

(3) A criminal bankruptcy order shall specify—

(*a*) the amount of the loss or damage appearing to the court to have resulted from the offence or, if more than one, each of the offences;

(*b*) the person or persons appearing to the court to have suffered that loss or damage;

(*c*) the amount of that loss or damage which it appears to the court that that person, or each of those persons, has suffered; and

(*d*) the date which is to be the relevant date for the purpose of the exercise by the High Court of its powers under paragraph 10 of Schedule 2 to this Act in relation to dispositions made by the offender, being the date which appears to the court to be the earliest date on which the offence or, if more than one, the earliest of the offences, was committed.

(4) A criminal bankruptcy order may be made against two or more offenders in respect of the same loss or damage.

(5) Schedule 2 to this Act shall have effect in relation to criminal bankruptcy orders and the operation of the enactments relating to bankruptcy in a case where such an order has been made, and also for supplementing those enactments in relation to dispositions made by an offender against whom such an order has been made.

PART I

(6) The Secretary of State may by order direct that subsection (1) above shall be amended by substituting, for the amount specified in that subsection as originally enacted or as previously amended under this subsection, such amount as may be specified in the order.

Appeals in the case of criminal bankruptcy orders.

40.—(1) No appeal shall lie against the making of a criminal bankruptcy order.

(2) Where a person successfully appeals to the Court of Appeal against his conviction of an offence by virtue of which such an order was made, the court shall rescind the order unless he was convicted in the same proceedings of another offence of which he remains convicted and a criminal bankruptcy order could have been made without reference to loss or damage caused by the first-mentioned offence; and where, accordingly, it does not rescind the order it shall amend it by striking out so much of it as relates to such loss or damage.

(3) Where on an appeal by a person against his conviction of an offence by virtue of which a criminal bankruptcy order was made the Court of Appeal substitutes a verdict of guilty of another offence, the court shall—

(*a*) rescind the order if a criminal bankruptcy order could not have been made against that person if he had originally been convicted of that other offence;

(*b*) in any other case, amend the order so far as may be required in consequence of the substitution of a verdict of guilty of the other offence.

(4) Where the Court of Appeal rescinds or amends a criminal bankruptcy order, the rescission or amendment shall not take effect—

(*a*) in any case until the expiration of the time for applying for leave to appeal to the House of Lords against the Court of Appeal's decision on the appeal against conviction (disregarding any extension of time which may be granted under section 34 of the Criminal Appeal Act 1968);

1968 c. 19.

(*b*) if an application for leave to appeal is made within that time, so long as an appeal to the House of Lords is pending; and

(*c*) if on such an appeal the conviction is restored by that House.

(5) For the purposes of this section an appeal to the House of Lords shall be treated as pending until any application for leave to appeal is disposed of and, if leave to appeal is granted, until the appeal is disposed of; and for the purposes of this

subsection an application for leave to appeal shall be treated as disposed of at the expiration of the time within which it may be made if it is not made within that time. PART I

The Official Petitioner.

41.—(1) For the purpose of discharging, in relation to cases in which a criminal bankruptcy order is made, the functions assigned to him by Schedule 2 to this Act, there shall continue to be an officer known as the Official Petitioner; and the Director of Public Prosecutions shall, by virtue of his office, continue to be the Official Petitioner.

(2) Neither the Official Petitioner nor any person acting under his authority shall be liable to any action or proceeding in respect of anything done or omitted in the discharge, or purported discharge, of the functions of the Official Petitioner under or by virtue of this Act.

(3) Any expenses of the Official Petitioner shall be defrayed out of moneys provided by Parliament.

Miscellaneous Powers

Power of Crown Court on committal for sentence. 1952 c. 55. 1967 c. 80.

42. Where an offender is committed by a magistrates' court for sentence under section 29 of the Magistrates' Courts Act 1952 or section 62 of the Criminal Justice Act 1967, the Crown Court shall enquire into the circumstances of the case and shall have power to deal with the offender in any manner in which it could deal with him if he had just been convicted of the offence on indictment before the court.

Power to deprive offender of property used, or intended for use, for purposes of crime.

43.—(1) Where a person is convicted of an offence punishable on indictment with imprisonment for a term of two years or more and the court by or before which he is convicted is satisfied that any property which was in his possession or under his control at the time of his apprehension—

(*a*) has been used for the purpose of committing, or facilitating the commission of, any offence; or

(*b*) was intended by him to be used for that purpose;

the court may make an order under this section in respect of that property.

(2) Facilitating the commission of an offence shall be taken for the purposes of this section and section 44 of this Act to include the taking of any steps after it has been committed for the purpose of disposing of any property to which it relates or of avoiding apprehension or detection, and references in this or that section to an offence punishable with imprisonment shall be construed without regard to any prohibition or restriction imposed by or under any enactment on the imprisonment of young offenders.

PART I

(3) An order under this section shall operate to deprive the offender of his rights, if any, in the property to which it relates, and the property shall (if not already in their possession) be taken into the possession of the police.

1897 c. 30.

(4) The Police (Property) Act 1897 shall apply, with the following modifications, to property which is in the possession of the police by virtue of this section—

(*a*) no application shall be made under section 1(1) of that Act by any claimant of the property after the expiration of six months from the date on which the order in respect of the property was made under this section; and

(*b*) no such application shall succeed unless the claimant satisfies the court either that he had not consented to the offender having possession of the property or that he did not know, and had no reason to suspect, that the property was likely to be used for the purpose mentioned in subsection (1) above.

(5) In relation to property which is in the possession of the police by virtue of this section, the power to make regulations under section 2(1) of the Police (Property) Act 1897 (disposal of property in cases where the owner of the property has not been ascertained and no order of a competent court has been made with respect thereto) shall include power to make regulations for disposal in cases where no application by a claimant of the property has been made within the period specified in subsection (4)(*a*) above or no such application has succeeded.

Driving disqualification where vehicle used for purposes of crime.

1952 c. 55.

44.—(1) This section applies where a person is convicted before the Crown Court of an offence punishable on indictment with imprisonment for a term of two years or more or, having been convicted by a magistrates' court of such an offence, is committed under section 29 of the Magistrates' Courts Act 1952 to the Crown Court for sentence.

(2) If in a case to which this section applies the Crown Court is satisfied that a motor vehicle was used (by the person convicted or by anyone else) for the purpose of committing, or facilitating the commission of, the offence in question (within the meaning of section 43 of this Act), the court may order the person convicted to be disqualified, for such period as the court thinks fit, for holding or obtaining a licence to drive a motor vehicle granted under Part III of the Road Traffic Act 1972.

1972 c. 20.

(3) A court which makes an order under this section disqualifying a person for holding or obtaining any such licence

as is mentioned in subsection (2) above shall require him to produce any such licence held by him ; and— PART I

(*a*) if he does not produce the licence as required he shall be guilty of an offence under section 101(4) of the Road Traffic Act 1972 (failure to produce licence for endorsement) ; and 1972 c. 20.

(*b*) if he applies under section 95 of that Act for the disqualification to be removed and the court so orders, subsection (4) of that section shall not have effect so as to require particulars of the order to be endorsed on the licence, but the court shall send notice of the order to the Secretary of State and section 105(5) of that Act (procedure for sending notice to Secretary of State) shall apply to the notice.

Supplemental

Social inquiry report before sentence.

45.—(1) The Secretary of State may by rules make provision requiring that in any case to which the rules apply a court of any prescribed class shall before passing on any person a sentence to which the rules apply consider a social inquiry report, that is to say a report about him and his circumstances, made by a probation officer or any other person authorised to do so by the rules.

(2) Rules under this section may apply to a sentence of imprisonment or detention of any class prescribed by the rules and may make different provision for different cases.

(3) No sentence shall be invalidated by the failure of a court to consider a social inquiry report in accordance with rules under subsection (1) above, but any other court on appeal from that court shall consider such a report in determining whether a different sentence should be passed on the appellant from the sentence passed on him by the court below.

(4) In this section " sentence of imprisonment or detention " means a sentence of imprisonment, Borstal training or detention in a detention centre or a sentence of detention passed under section 53 of the Children and Young Persons Act 1933 (young offenders convicted of grave crimes). 1933 c. 12.

Reports of probation officers.

46.—(1) Subject to subsection (2) below, where a report by a probation officer is made to any court (other than a juvenile court) with a view to assisting the court in determining the most suitable method of dealing with any person in respect of an offence, a copy of the report shall be given by the court to the offender or his counsel or solicitor.

(2) If the offender is under seventeen years of age and is not represented by counsel or a solicitor, a copy of the report need not be given to him but shall be given to his parent or guardian if present in court.

PART II

ADMINISTRATIVE AND SUPPLEMENTAL PROVISIONS

Rehabilitation of offenders and arrangements for persons on bail

The probation and after-care service and its functions.

47. The provisions of Schedule 3 to this Act shall have effect with respect to the probation and after-care service and its functions and matters connected therewith and, in particular (but without prejudice to the generality of the preceding provision), with respect to—

(*a*) the constitution of probation and after-care areas and of probation and after-care committees and case committees ;

(*b*) the appointment, functions, remuneration and conditions of service of probation officers ;

(*c*) the making of arrangements for persons to perform work under community service orders ; and

(*d*) the provision and carrying on of day training centres and other establishments for use in connection with the rehabilitation of offenders.

Power of Secretary of State to regulate community service work and training at day training centres.

48.—(1) The Secretary of State may make rules for regulating the performance of work under community service orders and the arrangements made under Schedule 3 to this Act for persons to perform such work.

(2) Without prejudice to the generality of subsection (1) above, rules under this section may in particular—

(*a*) limit the number of hours' work to be done by a person under such an order on any one day ;

(*b*) make provision as to the reckoning of time worked under such orders ;

(*c*) make provision for the payment of travelling and other expenses in connection with the performance of work under such orders ;

(*d*) provide for records to be kept of the work done by any person under such an order.

(3) The Secretary of State may make rules for regulating the training given at day training centres and the provision and carrying on of such centres under Schedule 3 to this Act ; and,

without prejudice to the generality of the preceding provision, such rules may in particular— PART II

(*a*) regulate the hours of attendance, and the reckoning of days of attendance, at such centres;

(*b*) provide for records to be kept of such attendance;

(*c*) provide that no person shall be appointed to be in charge of such a centre unless the Secretary of State has consented to his appointment.

(4) References in subsection (3) above to attendance at a day training centre include references to attendance elsewhere than at the centre for the purpose of receiving training in accordance with instructions given by, or under the authority of, the person in charge of the centre.

Power of Secretary of State to approve bail hostels and probation hostels and homes.

49.—(1) The Secretary of State may approve bail hostels, probation hostels and probation homes, and probation hostels and homes so approved shall be known respectively as approved probation hostels and approved probation homes.

(2) The Secretary of State may make rules for the regulation, management and inspection of approved bail hostels, approved probation hostels and approved probation homes; and such rules may in particular (subject to subsection (3) below) provide that no person shall be appointed to be in charge of any such hostel or home unless the Secretary of State has consented to his appointment.

(3) Rules made by the Secretary of State under subsection (2) above shall not prohibit the appointment of a person to be in charge of any such hostel or home in case of emergency without the previous consent of the Secretary of State, but may in that case require notice of the appointment to be given immediately to the Secretary of State and enable him, if he thinks fit, to require the appointment to be terminated.

Inspection of approved bail hostels and of non-approved institutions for residence of probationers.

50.—(1) Any approved bail hostel and, subject to subsection (2) below, any institution in which a person is required by a probation order to reside otherwise than for the purpose of his submitting to treatment for his mental condition as a resident patient shall be subject to inspection by the Secretary of State unless it is, as a whole, otherwise subject to inspection by a Government department.

(2) Subsection (1) above does not apply to an approved probation hostel or home, and applies to an institution in which a person is required as mentioned in that subsection to reside only so long as he resides there.

PART II

(3) A person appointed by the Secretary of State to inspect any approved bail hostel or any institution to which subsection (1) above applies shall have power to enter the hostel or institution and to make such investigation of the treatment of any persons residing there as he thinks fit; and any person who obstructs him in the exercise of that power shall be liable on summary conviction to a fine not exceeding £5.

Expenses and grants

Expenses and grants payable out of moneys provided by Parliament.

51.—(1) Any expenses of the Secretary of State under this Part of this Act, and any expenses incurred by the Secretary of State—

(*a*) in the training of probation officers or of officers or servants serving in approved probation hostels or homes, or of persons for appointment as probation officers, or as officers or servants in such hostels or homes; or

(*b*) in the conduct of research into the causes of delinquency and the treatment of offenders, and matters connected therewith;

shall, to such amount as may be sanctioned by the Treasury, be defrayed out of moneys provided by Parliament.

(2) The Secretary of State may with the approval of the Treasury provide for the making of payments towards the cost of the maintenance of persons attending at day training centres and their dependants.

(3) There shall be paid out of moneys provided by Parliament—

(*a*) towards the expenditure of local authorities, and the expenditure out of the metropolitan police fund, under Schedule 3 to this Act;

(*b*) towards the expenditure of probation and after-care committees in providing and carrying on, under paragraph 11 of that Schedule, bail hostels, probation hostels and probation homes;

(*c*) towards the expenditure of any society or person in enlarging, improving or carrying on bail hostels or approved probation hostels or homes or establishing, enlarging or improving premises which, when established, enlarged or improved, will be bail hostels or approved probation hostels or homes;

(*d*) towards the expenditure of any body approved by the Secretary of State in the training of probation officers or of persons for appointment as probation officers;

PART II

(e) towards the expenditure of any body approved by the Secretary of State in the training of officers or servants serving in any place in which offenders or persons awaiting trial may be detained or serving in approved probation hostels or homes or the training of persons for appointment as such officers or servants;

(f) towards the expenditure of any society or individual engaged in supervising or assisting persons convicted of offences with a view to their rehabilitation;

(g) towards the expenditure of any body or person approved by the Secretary of State in the conduct of research into the causes of delinquency and the treatment of offenders, and matters connected therewith;

such sums as the Secretary of State may with the approval of the Treasury direct, and subject to such conditions as he may with the like approval determine.

(4) Subject to subsection (5) below, the Secretary of State may, with the consent of the Treasury, make regulations providing for the deduction from any sums which would otherwise be paid out of moneys provided by Parliament to local authorities, whether under subsection (3) above or under the Children and Young Persons Act 1933, of such amounts as may be prescribed by the regulations in respect of expenditure incurred by the Secretary of State— 1933 c. 12.

(a) in the training of any such officers, servants or other persons as are mentioned in subsection (1) above;

(b) in making any payments under paragraph (c) or (d) of subsection (3) above;

(c) in making payments under paragraph (e) of subsection (3) above in respect of expenditure incurred in the training of officers or servants serving in approved probation hostels or homes or the training of persons for appointment as such officers or servants.

(5) The sums to be deducted in respect of any expenditure of the Secretary of State in pursuance of any regulations made under subsection (4) above shall not exceed half that expenditure.

(6) The conditions subject to which any sums are paid to a probation and after-care committee under paragraph (b) of subsection (3) above may include conditions for securing the repayment in whole or in part of the sums received by the committee if the hostel or home in question ceases to be used as such.

(7) The conditions subject to which any sums are paid to any society or person under paragraph (c) of subsection (3) above

PART II

may include conditions for securing the repayment in whole or in part of the sums received by the society or person—

(*a*) where the sums are paid in respect of a bail hostel, if it ceases to be used as such;

(*b*) where the sums are paid in respect of an approved probation hostel or home, if it ceases to be approved;

and, notwithstanding anything in the constitution of the hostel or home in question or of the managers thereof, or in the trusts, if any, to which the property of the hostel or home or of the managers is subject, the managers and any persons who are trustees of any of the property in question may accept those sums on those conditions, and execute any instrument required for carrying into effect those conditions, and shall be bound by those conditions and by any instrument so executed and have power to fulfil the conditions and the obligations created by the instrument.

(8) All sums received by the Secretary of State under this section shall be paid into the Consolidated Fund.

Miscellaneous and supplemental

Evidence with respect to offences punishable in Scotland.

52. For the purposes of this Act a certificate purporting to be signed by or on behalf of the Lord Advocate that an offence is punishable in Scotland with imprisonment or is punishable in Scotland on indictment with imprisonment for a term specified in the certificate shall be evidence of the matter so certified.

Execution of process between England and Wales and Scotland. 1881 c. 24 1949 c. 94 1952 c. 55

53. Section 4 of the Summary Jurisdiction (Process) Act 1881 (execution of process of English courts in Scotland and vice versa) shall apply to any process issued under Part I of this Act or under section 5 of the Criminal Justice (Scotland) Act 1949 as it applies to process issued under the Magistrates' Courts Act 1952 by a magistrates' court.

Rules and orders.

54.—(1) Any power of the Secretary of State to make rules or orders under this Act shall be exercised by statutory instrument.

(2) Subject to subsection (3) below, any rules or orders made by the Secretary of State under this Act shall be subject to annulment in pursuance of a resolution of either House of Parliament.

(3) Subsection (2) above does not apply to rules under section 49 of this Act nor to orders under section 14 of or paragraph 1 of Schedule 3 to this Act, but no order shall be made by the Secretary of State under section 14 unless a draft of it has been laid before, and approved by a resolution of, each House of Parliament.

PART II

(4) Any order made by the Secretary of State under section 14 or 39 of this Act may be revoked by a subsequent order of the Secretary of State under that section, an order under section 26(2)(*a*) may be revoked by a subsequent order under that paragraph or under section 26(2)(*b*), and an order under paragraph 1 of Schedule 3 to this Act may be varied or revoked by a subsequent order.

Transitional provisions.

55. Schedule 4 to this Act shall have effect for the purpose of the transition to the provisions of this Act from the law in force before the commencement of this Act.

Consequential amendments and repeals.

56.—(1) The enactments specified in Schedule 5 to this Act shall have effect subject to the amendments set out in that Schedule, being amendments consequential on the preceding provisions of this Act, but the amendment of any enactment by that Schedule shall not be taken as prejudicing the operation of section 38 of the Interpretation Act 1889 (which relates to the effect of repeals). 1889 c. 63.

(2) The enactments specified in Schedule 6 to this Act (which include enactments which were spent before the passing of this Act) are hereby repealed to the extent specified in the third column of that Schedule.

Interpretation.

57.—(1) In this Act, except so far as the context otherwise requires, the following expressions have the meanings hereby respectively assigned to them, that is to say—

" the appropriate officer of the court " means, in relation to a magistrates' court, the clerk of the court ;

" approved bail hostel " means a bail hostel approved by the Secretary of State under section 49(1) of this Act ;

" approved probation hostel " and " approved probation home " mean respectively a probation hostel and a probation home approved by the Secretary of State under section 49(1) of this Act ;

" bail hostel " means premises for the accommodation of persons remanded on bail ;

" community service order " has the meaning assigned to it by section 14(1) of this Act ;

" compensation order " has the meaning assigned to it by section 35(1) of this Act ;

" court " does not include a court-martial ;

" criminal bankruptcy order " means an order under section 39(1) of this Act ;

PART II

" day training centre " means premises at which persons may be required to attend by a probation order containing a requirement under section 4 of this Act;

1952 c. 52.

" detention centre " has the meaning assigned to it by section 43 of the Prison Act 1952;

" extended sentence certificate " has the meaning assigned to it by section 28 of this Act;

" local authority " means, in relation to any probation and after-care area, any authority out of whose funds the salary of the clerk to the justices for a petty sessions area contained in the probation and after-care area is paid;

" order for conditional discharge " has the meaning assigned to it by section 7 of this Act;

" period of conditional discharge " has the meaning assigned to it by section 7 of this Act;

" probationer " means a person for the time being under supervision by virtue of a probation order;

" probation hostel " means premises for the accommodation of persons who may be required to reside there by a probation order, being persons who are employed outside the premises or are awaiting such employment, and " probation home " has the same meaning save only that the premises are for the accommodation of persons not so employed or awaiting such employment;

" probation order " has the meaning assigned to it by section 2 of this Act;

" probation period " means the period for which a probationer is placed under supervision by a probation order;

1949 c. 101.

" the register " means the register of proceedings before a magistrates' court required by rules made under section 15 of the Justices of the Peace Act 1949 to be kept by the clerk of the court;

" sentence of imprisonment " does not include a committal in default of payment of any sum of money, or for want of sufficient distress to satisfy any sum of money, or for failure to do or abstain from doing anything required to be done or left undone;

" supervising court " has the meaning assigned to it by section 2(2) of this Act;

PART II

"supervision order" has the meaning assigned to it by section 26(1) of this Act;

"suspended sentence" means a sentence to which an order under section 22(1) of this Act relates.

(2) For the purposes of any reference in this Act, however expressed, to the term of imprisonment or other detention to which a person has been sentenced or which, or part of which, he has served, consecutive terms and terms which are wholly or partly concurrent shall, unless the context otherwise requires, be treated as a single term.

(3) Without prejudice to sections 20(1) and 21(1) of this Act, any reference in this Act however expressed to a previous conviction or sentence shall be construed as a reference to a previous conviction by a court in any part of Great Britain and to a previous sentence passed by any such court.

(4) Without prejudice to the meaning of references in sections 14, 43 and 44 of this Act to an offence punishable with imprisonment, any such reference elsewhere in this Act shall be construed, in relation to any offender, without regard to any prohibition or restriction imposed by or under any enactment on the imprisonment of offenders of his age.

(5) For the purposes of this Act a compensation order, supervision order or community service order made on appeal from a decision of a magistrates' court or the Crown Court shall be treated as if it had been made by a magistrates' court or the Crown Court, as the case may be.

(6) Any reference in this Act to any other enactment is a reference thereto as amended, and includes a reference thereto as extended or applied, by or under any other enactment, including this Act.

Application to Scotland.

58. The following provisions of this Act shall extend to Scotland, that is to say—

(*a*) sections 8(4), 10, 13, 25(3), 29(7), 33, 53 and this section; and

(*b*) section 56 and Schedules 5 and 6 so far as they amend or repeal any enactment or any part of an enactment which extends to Scotland;

but, except as provided by this section, this Act shall not extend to Scotland.

Northern Ireland.

59.—(1) Section 29(7) of this Act and this section shall extend to Northern Ireland but except as provided by this subsection this Act shall not extend to Northern Ireland.

PART II

1920 c. 67. 1973 c. 36. 1972 c. 22.

(2) For the purposes of section 6 of the Government of Ireland Act 1920, in so far as, notwithstanding its repeal by the Northern Ireland Constitution Act 1973, it continues to operate in relation to the power of Her Majesty to make laws under section 1(3) of the Northern Ireland (Temporary Provisions) Act 1972, section 29(7) of this Act shall be deemed to be a provision of an Act passed before the appointed day within the meaning of that section.

1961 c. 39.

(3) The references in section 29(6) and (7) of this Act to section 26 of the Criminal Justice Act 1961 shall be construed, in relation to Northern Ireland, as references to that section as amended by any Act of the Parliament of Northern Ireland, or Measure of the Northern Ireland Assembly, whether passed before or after this Act.

1972 c. 71.

(4) Nothing in any repeal made by this Act shall affect any power exercisable by Her Majesty by virtue of section 63(1) of the Criminal Justice Act 1972 (notwithstanding its repeal by the Northern Ireland Constitution Act 1973) to make laws under section 1(3) of the Northern Ireland (Temporary Provisions) Act 1972 for purposes corresponding to any of the purposes of the Criminal Justice Act 1972 as originally enacted.

Short title and commencement.

60.—(1) This Act may be cited as the Powers of Criminal Courts Act 1973.

(2) This Act shall come into force on such day as the Secretary of State may by order appoint, and different days may be so appointed for different provisions; and any reference in any provision of this Act to the commencement of this Act shall be construed as a reference to the day so appointed for the coming into force of that provision.

SCHEDULES

SCHEDULE 1

Section 5.

Discharge and Amendment of Probation Orders

Discharge

1.—(1) A probation order may be discharged, in accordance with the following provisions of this paragraph, on an application made by the probation officer or by the probationer.

(2) Where the probation order was made by the court by or before which the probationer was convicted, or on appeal, the power to discharge the order shall, subject to sub-paragraph (3) below, be exercised by the supervising court.

(3) Where the court before which the probationer was convicted or the court from which the appeal is brought is the Crown Court and there is included in the order a direction that the power be reserved to that court, the power to discharge the order shall be exercised by the Crown Court.

(4) In any other case the power to discharge the order shall be exercised by the court by which the order was made.

Amendment

2.—(1) Subject to sub-paragraph (2) below, if the supervising court is satisfied that a probationer proposes to change, or has changed his residence from the petty sessions area named in the probation order to another petty sessions area, the court may, and on the application of the probation officer shall, by order amend the probation order by substituting for the petty sessions area named in the order the petty sessions area where the probationer proposes to reside or is residing.

(2) If the probation order contains requirements which, in the opinion of the court, cannot be complied with unless the probationer continues to reside in the area named in the order, the court shall not amend the order under this paragraph unless, in accordance with the following provisions of this Schedule, it cancels those requirements or substitutes for those requirements other requirements which can be complied with if the probationer ceases to reside in that area.

(3) Where a probation order is amended under this paragraph, the old supervising court shall send to the clerk to the justices for the new area named in the order a copy of the order, together with such documents and information relating to the case as it considers likely to be of assistance to the new supervising court.

3.—(1) Without prejudice to the provisions of paragraph 2 above, but subject to sub-paragraph (2) below, the supervising court may, on an application made by the probation officer or by the probationer, by order amend a probation order by cancelling any of the requirements of the order or by inserting in the order (either in addition to or in substitution for any such requirement) any require-

SCH. 1 ment which the court could include under section 2, 3 or 4 of this Act if it were then making the order.

(2) The power of the supervising court under this paragraph to amend a probation order shall be subject to the following restrictions—

(*a*) the court shall not amend a probation order by reducing the probation period, or by extending that period beyond the end of three years from the date of the original order;

(*b*) the court shall not so amend a probation order that the probationer is thereby required to reside in an approved probation hostel or home or in any other institution for any period exceeding twelve months in all;

(*c*) the court shall not amend a probation order by inserting therein a requirement that the probationer shall submit to treatment for his mental condition unless the amending order is made within three months after the date of the original order.

4. Where the medical practitioner by whom or under whose direction a probationer is being treated for his mental condition in pursuance of any requirement of the probation order is of opinion—

(*a*) that the treatment of the probationer should be continued beyond the period specified in that behalf in the order, or

(*b*) that the probationer needs different treatment, being treatment of a kind to which he could be required to submit in pursuance of a probation order, or

(*c*) that the probationer is not susceptible to treatment, or

(*d*) that the probationer does not require further treatment,

or where the practitioner is for any reason unwilling to continue to treat or direct the treatment of the probationer, he shall make a report in writing to that effect to the probation officer and the probation officer shall apply to the supervising court for the variation or cancellation of the requirement.

General

5.—(1) Subject to sub-paragraph (2) below, where the supervising court proposes to amend a probation order under this Schedule, otherwise than on the application of the probationer, it shall summon him to appear before the court; and the court shall not amend a probation order unless the probationer expresses his willingness to comply with the requirements of the order as amended.

(2) This paragraph shall not apply to an order cancelling a requirement of the probation order or reducing the period of any requirement, or substituting a new petty sessions area for the area named in the probation order.

6.—(1) On the making of an order discharging or amending a probation order, the clerk to the court shall forthwith—

(*a*) if the order discharges the probation order or amends it otherwise than by substituting a new petty sessions area for the area named in the probation order, give copies of the discharging or amending order to the probation officer ;

(b) if the order amends the probation order in the manner excepted by head (a) above, send copies of the amending order to the clerk to the justices for the new petty sessions area ;

and in a case falling within head (b) above the clerk to the justices for the new petty sessions area shall give copies of the amending order to the probation officer.

(2) A probation officer to whom in accordance with sub-paragraph (1) above copies of an order are given shall give a copy to the probationer and to the person in charge of any institution in which the probationer is or was required by the order to reside.

7. Section 2(8) of this Act shall apply to any order made under this Schedule by virtue of which a probationer is required to reside in an institution as it applies to a probation order made under that section.

SCHEDULE 2

Section 39.

Criminal Bankruptcy Orders

Part I

General

Act of bankruptcy

1. Subject to the provisions of this Schedule, where a criminal bankruptcy order is made against any person he shall be treated as a debtor who has committed an act of bankruptcy on the date on which the order is made.

Creditors and criminal bankruptcy debts

2. A person specified in a criminal bankruptcy order as having suffered loss or damage of any amount shall be treated, for the purpose of any ensuing proceedings pursuant to—

(a) a bankruptcy petition presented by virtue of paragraph 1 above ; or

(b) a petition under section 130 of the Bankruptcy Act 1914 (administration in bankruptcy of estate of deceased debtor) presented by virtue of this Schedule ; 1914 c. 59.

as a creditor for a debt of that amount provable in the bankruptcy of the person against whom the order was made.

Rules

3. For the purposes of section 132 of the Bankruptcy Act 1914 (general rules for carrying the objects of that Act into effect) this Schedule, except paragraphs 8 and 10, shall be deemed to be part of that Act.

SCH. 2

Interpretation

4. In Parts II and III of this Schedule—

1914 c. 59. "the Act of 1914" means the Bankruptcy Act 1914;

"criminal bankruptcy petition" means any such petition as is mentioned in paragraph 2(*a*) above and "criminal bankruptcy administration petition" means any such petition as is mentioned in paragraph 2(*b*) above; and

"criminal bankruptcy debt" means a debt deemed to be due to any person by virtue of paragraph 2 above.

PART II

PROCEEDINGS BASED ON A CRIMINAL BANKRUPTCY ORDER: APPLICATION OF THE ACT OF 1914, ETC.

Criminal bankruptcy petition

5.—(1) A criminal bankruptcy petition shall be presented to the High Court, but without prejudice to any power of transferring bankruptcy proceedings to any other court.

(2) No criminal bankruptcy petition shall be presented by the person who under paragraph 1 above is the debtor; and, in relation to such a petition presented by a creditor, section 4 of the Act of 1914 shall have effect with the following modifications—

(*a*) subsections (1)(*a*) and (*b*) and (2) (conditions as to nature of debt) shall not apply to a criminal bankruptcy debt; and

(*b*) subsection (1)(*d*) (domicile of debtor) shall be omitted.

Receiving order

6. For the purposes of section 5(2) and (3) of the Act of 1914 (matters to be proved before receiving order is made) the act of bankruptcy which a person is treated by this Schedule as having committed and any criminal bankruptcy debt shall be treated as conclusively proved by the production of a copy of the criminal bankruptcy order in question, and subsections (5) and (6) of that section shall not apply in relation to any such debt.

7. Section 12 of the Act of 1914 (power to rescind receiving order to enable bankruptcy proceedings to proceed in Scotland or Northern Ireland) shall not apply to a receiving order made on a criminal bankruptcy petition.

Trustee of criminal bankrupt's property

8. Where a person is adjudged bankrupt in proceedings pursuant to a criminal bankruptcy petition the official receiver (and not a person appointed under section 19 of the Act of 1914) shall in the bankruptcy be trustee of the property of the bankrupt.

Sch. 2

Proof of criminal bankruptcy debt in bankruptcy proceedings

9.—(1) For the purpose of proving a criminal bankruptcy debt in proceedings pursuant to a criminal bankruptcy petition, a copy of the criminal bankruptcy order specifying the amount deemed by virtue of paragraph 2 above to be due as a debt shall, subject to paragraph 6 above, be treated as sufficient evidence of the debt unless it is shown by any party to the proceedings that the amount of the relevant loss or damage is greater or less than the amount specified in the order or that the loss or damage did not in fact result from any offence specified in the order ; and if it is shown by any party to the proceedings that the amount of the relevant loss or damage is greater than that specified in the order, paragraph 2 above shall have effect as if the greater amount had been specified in the order.

(2) Nothing in this paragraph or paragraph 2 above shall be taken as prejudicing the proof in proceedings pursuant to a criminal bankruptcy petition of debts other than criminal bankruptcy debts.

(3) Nothing in sub-paragraph (1) above shall be construed as entitling any person to contend that the offence or offences specified in a criminal bankruptcy order were not committed by the person against whom the order was made.

Recovery of assets for benefit of criminal bankrupt's creditors

10.—(1) Without prejudice to any provision of the Act of 1914, the following provisions of this paragraph shall apply, where a person is adjudged bankrupt in proceedings pursuant to a criminal bankruptcy petition, with respect to dispositions of property or any interest in property made by the bankrupt on or after the relevant date, either by way of gift or for an under-value.

In this sub-paragraph, " the relevant date " means the date specified in the order (in accordance with section 39(3)(*d*) of this Act) as the earliest date on which the offence or, as the case may be, the earliest of the offences, was committed.

(2) On the application of the official receiver (in his capacity as trustee) the High Court may make orders requiring—

(*a*) the person taking under any such disposition ; or

(*b*) subject to the following sub-paragraph, any other person who by virtue of any subsequent disposition acquired (whether or not from the person taking under the bankrupt's disposition) the whole or any part of the property or any interest therein ;

to transfer the whole or any part of the property, or such interest as the order may specify, to the trustee, or to make such payments to the trustee as the court thinks just with a view to making available to the creditors the full value of the property or interest disposed of by the bankrupt (including any increase in its value since the disposition was made).

(3) No order shall be made by virtue of sub-paragraph (2)(*b*) above against a person appearing to the court to have given full value for anything taken by him under a relevant disposition or to claim (directly or indirectly) through a person who gave full value.

SCH. 2

(4) An order of the High Court under this paragraph requiring a person to transfer any property or interest may include such consequential directions for giving effect to the order, and be made on such terms (including in particular terms allowing the person to retain or recover consideration given by him for any relevant disposition) as the court thinks just in all the circumstances.

(5) In this paragraph " disposition " includes any conveyance or assurance of property of any description.

Administration in bankruptcy of deceased offender's estate

11.—(1) Paragraph 5(1) above shall apply to a criminal bankruptcy administration petition as it applies to a criminal bankruptcy petition.

(2) Where an order for administration is made under section 130 of the Act of 1914 on a criminal bankruptcy administration petition, so much of subsection (4) of that section as enables the creditors to appoint a trustee of the property of the debtor in place of the official receiver shall not apply.

(3) Paragraph 9 above shall apply in relation to proof of criminal bankruptcy debts in proceedings pursuant to a criminal bankruptcy administration petition as it applies in relation to proof of such debts in proceedings pursuant to a criminal bankruptcy petition.

Bankruptcy proceedings otherwise than by virtue of this Schedule

12. Where a criminal bankruptcy order has been made against any person and a bankruptcy petition has been presented in respect of him before the order was made, or is presented in respect of him thereafter otherwise than by virtue of paragraph 1 above, the court having jurisdiction in relation to the bankruptcy may, on the application of the Official Petitioner, dismiss the petition, rescind any receiving order made in pursuance thereof or, if that person has been adjudged bankrupt, annul the adjudication on such terms, if any, as the court thinks fit.

Effect of appeal against conviction

13.—(1) Subject to the provisions of this paragraph, the fact that an appeal is pending against any conviction by virtue of which a criminal bankruptcy order was made shall not preclude the taking of any proceedings by virtue of this Schedule in consequence of the making of the order.

(2) Where a person is adjudged bankrupt in proceedings pursuant to a criminal bankruptcy petition, no property shall be distributed by his trustee in bankruptcy and no order shall be made by the High Court under paragraph 10 above so long as an appeal is pending against his conviction of any offence by virtue of which the criminal bankruptcy order was made.

(3) For the purposes of this paragraph an appeal against a conviction is pending—

(*a*) in any case until the expiration of the period of 28 days beginning with the date of conviction ;

(*b*) if notice of appeal to the Court of Appeal is given during that period and during that period the appellant notifies the official receiver thereof, until the determination of the appeal and thereafter for so long as an appeal to the House of Lords is pending within the meaning of section 40(5) of this Act. SCH. 2

(4) Where in consequence of an appeal a criminal bankruptcy order is rescinded—

(*a*) any bankruptcy petition based on the order shall lapse and any receiving order or adjudication of bankruptcy made in consequence thereof shall cease to have effect, but without prejudice to anything previously done thereunder;

(*b*) where any such adjudication ceases to have effect, the property of the person who was adjudicated bankrupt shall revert to him for all his estate or interest therein; and

(*c*) the court which had jurisdiction in relation to the bankruptcy may, on his application or on the application of the official receiver, by order give such directions, if any, as appear to the court to be necessary or desirable in consequence of the preceding provisions of this paragraph.

(5) Where in consequence of an appeal a criminal bankruptcy order is amended by the deletion of any amount specified therein as the loss or damage suffered by any person, paragraph 2 above shall not thereafter apply to that loss or damage but without prejudice to anything done before the amendment takes effect.

PART III

FUNCTIONS OF OFFICIAL PETITIONER

General

14. The functions of the Official Petitioner are as follows—

(*a*) to consider whether, in a case in which a criminal bankruptcy order is made, it is in the public interest that he should himself present a criminal bankruptcy petition;

(*b*) to present a criminal bankruptcy petition in any such case where he determines it is in the public interest for him to do so;

(*c*) to make payments, in such cases as he may determine, towards expenses incurred by other persons in connection with proceedings pursuant to a criminal bankruptcy petition or a criminal bankruptcy administration petition;

(*d*) to exercise, so far as he considers it to be in the public interest to do so, any of the powers conferred on him by this Schedule.

Presentation of criminal bankruptcy petition by Official Petitioner

15.—(1) The Official Petitioner may present a criminal bankruptcy petition, and a receiving order may be made on that petition.

Sch. 2

(2) Section 4 of the Act of 1914, as modified by paragraph 5(2) above, shall apply to a criminal bankruptcy petition presented by the Official Petitioner as it applies to a petition presented by a creditor, but the High Court may allow the petition to be presented later than required by subsection (1)(*c*) of that section.

(3) A criminal bankruptcy petition presented by the Official Petitioner shall be served in the manner prescribed by rules made under the Act of 1914.

(4) Section 5(2), (3) and (7) of the Act of 1914 (making of receiving order on, and withdrawal of, creditor's petition) shall apply also in relation to a criminal bankruptcy petition presented by the Official Petitioner but as if any reference to the debt of the petitioning creditor were a reference to any criminal bankruptcy debt within the meaning of this Schedule; and paragraph 6 above shall have effect in relation to section 5(2) and (3) as they apply by virtue of this paragraph.

Presentation of criminal bankruptcy administration petition by Official Petitioner

16.—(1) The Official Petitioner may present a petition under section 130 of the Act of 1914 in any case in which a creditor could do so by virtue of this Schedule, and an order may be made under that section on that petition.

(2) Section 130(2) shall have effect in relation to a petition presented by the Official Petitioner as if the reference to the petitioner's debt were a reference to any criminal bankruptcy debt within the meaning of this Schedule.

Participation of Official Petitioner in proceedings brought by virtue of this Schedule (whether by the Official Petitioner or by a creditor)

17.—(1) In the case of proceedings pursuant to a criminal bankruptcy petition or a criminal bankruptcy administration petition, the Official Petitioner shall be entitled—

(*a*) to attend any meeting of creditors and, before the meeting, to receive any notice or other document required to be sent before such a meeting to any creditor;

(*b*) to be a member of any committee of inspection appointed under section 20 of the Act of 1914, but not so as to count towards the number of members mentioned in subsection (2) or (9), or to be subject to removal under subsection (7), of that section;

(*c*) to be a party to any such proceedings before any court.

(2) In the case of proceedings pursuant to a criminal bankruptcy petition or a criminal bankruptcy administration petition, the provisions mentioned in sub-paragraph (3) below shall have effect as if any reference to a creditor, or to a creditor who has proved or tendered a proof, included a reference to the Official Petitioner.

(3) The provisions of the Act of 1914 referred to in sub-paragraph (2) above are sections 10 (appointment of special manager), 14(2) and (4) (debtor's statement of affairs), 15(4) and (8) (public examination of debtor), 16(5), (6) and (8) (compositions and schemes of arrangement), 26(7) (discharge of bankrupt), 37 (relation back of trustee's title), 74(1)(*e*) (report to creditors of debtor's proposal), 80 (appeal to court against act or decision of trustee), and 130(8) (effect of notice of creditor's petition under that section). SCH. 2

(4) Any functions of the Official Petitioner under or by virtue of this Act may be discharged on his behalf by any person acting with his authority.

SCHEDULE 3

Section 47.

THE PROBATION AND AFTER-CARE SERVICE AND ITS FUNCTIONS

PART I

THE PROBATION AND AFTER-CARE SERVICE

Probation and after-care areas

1.—(1) Subject to the following provisions of this paragraph, if the Secretary of State is of opinion, either upon consideration of proposals submitted to him by a magistrates' courts committee for a county or without any such proposals, that it is expedient that any two or more petty sessions areas should form one probation and after-care area, he may make an order to that effect; and the order may contain such incidental and consequential provisions as appear to the Secretary of State to be expedient for the purposes of the order.

(2) Before making an order under sub-paragraph (1) above the Secretary of State shall give to the justices acting for any petty sessions area affected by the order an opportunity of making to him any representations which they may desire to make with respect to the order, and shall consider any representations made by them.

(3) The Secretary of State shall make provision by order under sub-paragraph (1) above for combining in one probation and after-care area all of the petty sessional divisions of the inner London area.

(4) The City of London shall not be included in a probation and after-care area constituted by an order made under sub-paragraph (1) above.

(5) Every petty sessions area which is not included in a probation and after-care area by virtue of an order made under sub-paragraph (1) above shall itself constitute a probation and after-care area.

Probation and after-care committees

2.—(1) For every probation and after-care area there shall be a probation and after-care committee, which shall be a body corporate.

SCH. 3

(2) Subject to the following provisions of this paragraph and to the provisions of paragraphs 6 and 7 below, a probation and after-care committee for any area shall consist—

(*a*) if that area comprises more than one petty sessions area, of such number of justices as may be specified by the order under paragraph 1(1) above, appointed in the manner so specified by the justices acting for the several petty sessions areas comprised in that area ;

(*b*) if that area is one petty sessions area, of a prescribed number of justices appointed in the prescribed manner by the justices acting for that petty sessions area.

(3) Sub-paragraph (2) above shall not apply to the probation and after-care committee for the inner London area, but that committee shall, subject to the provisions of sub-paragraph (4) below and of paragraphs 6 and 7 below, consist—

(*a*) of such number of metropolitan stipendiary magistrates, nominated by the chief metropolitan stipendiary magistrate, as may be specified by the order under paragraph 1(1) above ;

(*b*) of such number as may be so specified of lay justices for the petty sessional divisions of the area, chosen, in such manner as may be so specified, by the lay justices for those divisions ;

(*c*) of such number as may be so specified of the members of the juvenile courts panel for the inner London area and the City of London, chosen in such manner as may be so specified.

(4) The Lord Chancellor may, if he thinks fit, appoint—

(*a*) one or more judges of the Crown Court (being judges of the High Court, Circuit judges or Recorders) ; and

(*b*) one or more justices with experience of sitting as members of the Crown Court ;

to be members of the probation and after-care committee for any area, and any person so appointed shall hold office in accordance with the terms of his appointment.

(5) Any contract made or other thing done by or on behalf of a probation and after-care committee before it became, by virtue of section 37 of the Justices of the Peace Act 1949, a body corporate, shall have effect as if made or done by or on behalf of the body corporate constituted by sub-paragraph (1) above.

3.—(1) It shall be the duty of every probation and after-care committee—

(*a*) to appoint sufficient probation officers for their probation and after-care area, subject, in the case of such classes or descriptions of probation officers as may be prescribed, to the approval of the appointment by the Secretary of State, and to ensure that at least one probation officer who is a man and one probation officer who is a woman shall be appointed for or assigned by the committee to each petty sessions area ;

Sch. 3

(*b*) to pay to the probation officers appointed for their area such remuneration, allowances and expenses as may be prescribed;

(*c*) to provide for the efficient carrying out of the work of probation officers;

(*d*) to make such payments and to such persons as may be prescribed in respect of persons under the supervision of probation officers, being persons required by a probation order to reside in any place otherwise than for the purpose of their submitting to treatment for their mental condition as resident patients; and

(*e*) to perform such other duties in connection with the work of probation officers as may be prescribed.

(2) A probation and after-care committee may, in such cases and in such manner as may be prescribed, give financial and other assistance to persons under the supervision of probation officers appointed for their area.

(3) A probation and after-care committee may, with the approval of the Secretary of State, delegate all or any of their functions to a sub-committee consisting of members of the committee and such other persons (if any) as may be co-opted to be members of the sub-committee; but so that the number of co-opted members of the sub-committee shall not exceed the number of its members who are members of the committee.

(4) Notwithstanding that, by virtue of paragraph 2(1) above, a probation and after-care committee is a body corporate, any provision applying to employees of justices shall, unless the contrary intention appears, apply to employees of a probation and after-care committee.

Case committees

4.—(1) For every petty sessions area outside the inner London area there shall be one or more committees, to be called "case committees", and every such committee shall, subject to paragraphs 6 and 7 below, consist—

(*a*) if the petty sessions area is a separate probation and after-care area, of the probation and after-care committee;

(*b*) in any other case, of a prescribed number of justices appointed by the justices acting for that petty sessions area.

(2) It shall be the duty of case committees for areas outside the inner London area to review the work of probation officers, and to perform such other duties in connection with the work of probation officers as may be prescribed.

(3) Rules made under this Schedule relating to the procedure of case committees may provide, as respects case committees for areas outside the inner London area, that some only of the members of a case committee shall be summoned to deal with any particular case or class of cases.

(4) A probation and after-care committee for any area outside the inner London area shall pay any expenses incurred in accordance

SCH. 3 with rules made by the Secretary of State under this Schedule by a case committee for a petty sessions area in their probation and after-care area, and any allowances under paragraph 13 below to members of any such committee.

5.—(1) The probation and after-care committee for the inner London area may appoint such case committees, constituted in such manner and for such areas within that area, as the probation and after-care committee may determine, and shall pay the expenses of any case committee appointed under this sub-paragraph.

(2) Any case committee appointed for an area within the inner London area shall exercise functions conferred on case committees for areas outside the inner London area by paragraph 4(2) above to such extent and in such cases as may be determined by the probation and after-care committee for the inner London area.

Co-option of members of probation and after-care committees and case committees

6.—(1) Subject to the provisions of this paragraph, any probation and after-care committee, and any case committee which is not a probation and after-care committee, may co-opt such number of persons as they think fit.

(2) The number of members co-opted under sub-paragraph (1) above shall not not exceed one-third of the number of members of the committee, and no person shall be so co-opted if he is a justice of the peace for any county in which the probation and after-care area or any part of it is situated, or which is wholly or partly comprised in that area.

(3) The reference in sub-paragraph (2) above to a county includes a reference to any London commission area within the meaning of the Administration of Justice Act 1964 and to the City of London; but nothing in this paragraph applies to any case committee for an area within the inner London area.

1964 c. 42.

7.—(1) Subject to the provisions of this paragraph, each probation and after-care committee and each case committee which is not a probation and after-care committee shall co-opt a suitable number of persons having knowledge or experience of the after-care of discharged offenders, and if it appears to the Secretary of State that any such committee has failed to carry out the preceding requirement, he may appoint to the committee such number of persons having the knowledge or experience required as he thinks fit.

(2) Without prejudice to sub-paragraph (2) of paragraph 6 above the number of persons who may be co-opted or appointed to any such committee under that sub-paragraph and sub-paragraph (1) above shall not exceed one-third of the number of members of the committee, and no person shall be co-opted or appointed under sub-paragraph (1) above if he is a justice of the peace.

(3) Nothing in this paragraph applies to any case committee for an area within the inner London area.

Probation officers SCH. 3

8.—(1) It shall be the duty of probation officers to supervise the probationers and other persons placed under their supervision and to advise, assist and befriend them, to inquire, in accordance with any directions of the court, into the circumstances or home surroundings of any person with a view to assisting the court in determining the most suitable method of dealing with his case, to advise, assist and befriend, in such cases and in such manner as may be prescribed, persons who have been released from custody and to perform such other duties as may be prescribed or may be imposed by any enactment or instrument.

(2) In sub-paragraph (1) above " enactment " includes an enactment contained in a local Act and " instrument " means an instrument having effect by virtue of an Act.

9. The probation officer who is to be responsible for the supervision of any probationer shall be selected under arrangements made by the probation and after-care committee for the probation and after-care area which includes the petty sessions area for the time being named in the order from among the probation officers appointed for or assigned to that petty sessions area ; and, if the probation officer so selected dies or is unable for any reason to carry out his duties, or if the case committee dealing with the case think it desirable that another officer should take his place, another probation officer shall be selected in like manner from among the probation officers appointed for or assigned to that petty sessions area.

PART II

FUNCTIONS IN RELATION TO THE REHABILITATION OF OFFENDERS

Functions of probation and after-care committees in relation to community service orders

10.—(1) A probation and after-care committee may, with the approval of the Secretary of State, secure that arrangements for persons to perform work under community service orders are made for their area or, if it comprises more than one petty sessions area, for any of the petty sessions areas it comprises.

(2) Where in pursuance of this paragraph a probation and after-care committee secure the making of such arrangements, they shall appoint a sub-committee (to be known as the " community service committee ") to superintend the working of the arrangements ; and the community service committee shall consist of—

(*a*) such members of the probation and after-care committee ; and

(*b*) such other persons (not being justices of the peace) ;

as may be appointed by the probation and after-care committee, but so that the number of persons appointed under head (*b*) above shall not exceed the number of those appointed under head (*a*).

SCH. 3

(3) For the purposes of any arrangements made in pursuance of this paragraph for the whole or any part of the area of a probation and after-care committee, that committee shall have power—

(*a*) to appoint such staff as the committee think requisite ;

(*b*) to provide accommodation, equipment, materials and transport ;

(*c*) to make payments to any society or body in respect of services rendered by them ;

(*d*) to defray travelling and other expenses in connection with the performance of work by persons in respect of whom community service orders are in force.

Provision of establishments for use in connection with the rehabilitation of offenders, etc.

11. A probation and after-care committee may, with the approval of the Secretary of State, provide and carry on day training centres, bail hostels, probation hostels, probation homes and other establishments for use in connection with the rehabilitation of offenders.

12.—(1) A probation and after-care committee shall make such payments and to such persons as may be prescribed in respect of persons accommodated in probation hostels, probation homes and bail hostels.

(2) A probation and after-care committee may, in such cases and in such manner as may be prescribed, give financial and other assistance to persons remanded on bail.

PART III

GENERAL PROVISIONS

Travelling and subsistence allowances

13.—(1) Subject to the provisions of this paragraph, a member of a probation and after-care committee or case committee shall be entitled—

(*a*) to receive payments at the prescribed rates by way of travelling allowance or subsistence allowance where expenditure on travelling or, as the case may be, on subsistence is necessarily incurred by him for the purpose of enabling him to perform any of his duties as a member of the committee ; and

(*b*) to receive payments at the prescribed rate by way of financial loss allowance where for that purpose he incurs any other expenditure to which he would not otherwise be subject or suffers any loss of earnings or of benefit under the National Insurance Acts 1965 to 1967 which he would otherwise have made or received.

(2) For the purposes of sub-paragraph (1) above, a person appointed to a community service committee under paragraph 10(2)(*b*) above shall be deemed to be a member of the probation and after-care committee by which he is appointed, and duties performed by a

person as a member of a community service committee shall be deemed to be performed by him as a member of the probation and after-care committee by which the community service committee is appointed. SCH. 3

(3) Sub-paragraph (1) above shall not apply in relation to a member of a case committee for an area within the inner London area.

Adjustment of expenses of probation and after-care committees inter se

14.—(1) Where a probation officer is appointed for more than one probation and after-care area, his salary and any expenses incurred by him or by a probation and after-care committee in respect of the performance of his duties, and any expenses incurred in respect of a superannuation allowance, gratuity or compensation payable to or in respect of him or any clerk appointed to assist him under any regulations under section 7 of the Superannuation Act 1972 shall 1972 c. 11. be apportioned between the probation and after-care committees for the several probation and after-care areas for which he is appointed, in such manner as may be agreed between the committees concerned after consultation with the local authorities which, by virtue of paragraph 15 below, are required to defray the expenses of those committees, or as in default of agreement may be determined by the Secretary of State.

(2) Where a probation and after-care committee arrange for a person in another committee's area to perform work under a community service order, the probation and after-care committee for the other area shall make to the first-mentioned committee such payments in respect of that person and the arrangements made for him as may be agreed between the committees concerned or as in default of agreement may be determined by the Secretary of State.

(3) A probation and after-care committee shall, in respect of any person under the supervision of a probation officer for their area who attends at a day training centre carried on by another committee, make to the other committee such payments as may be agreed between the committees concerned or as in default of agreement may be determined by the Secretary of State.

Expenses of probation and after-care committees to be borne by local authorities

15.—(1) Subject to sub-paragraph (2) below and to paragraph 16 below the sums required to meet—

(*a*) any expenses incurred by a probation and after-care committee under the provisions of this Schedule (including allowances under paragraph 13);

(*b*) any expenses incurred by a probation and after-care committee in respect of superannuation allowances, gratuities or compensation payable by virtue of regulations under section 7 of the Superannuation Act 1972 to or in respect of probation officers and clerks appointed by probation and after-care committees or probation officers to assist probation officers in the performance of their duties; and

SCH. 3

(*c*) any other expenses incurred by a probation and after-care committee in accordance with rules made under this Schedule ;

shall be defrayed, in accordance with rules so made, by the local authority in whose area the probation and after-care area is situated.

(2) Sub-paragraph (1) above shall not apply to any expenses incurred by a probation and after-care committee in providing and carrying on probation hostels, probation homes and bail hostels.

(3) Where a probation and after-care area is situated in the area of two or more local authorities, the sums to be defrayed under sub-paragraph (1) above shall be apportioned between the several authorities in such manner as may be agreed between them or as in default of agreement may be determined by the Secretary of State.

1964 c. 42.

(4) Any expenditure incurred by virtue of this paragraph in relation to a probation and after-care area in any outer London area (within the meaning of the Administration of Justice Act 1964) by the Greater London Council shall be chargeable only on the outer London boroughs.

Special provision for expenses of the probation and after-care committee for the inner London area

16. Paragraph 15 above shall not apply in relation to expenses incurred by the probation and after-care committee for the inner London area, but there shall be paid out of the metropolitan police fund such sums as the Secretary of State may direct to meet the expenses and contributions which, in the case of a probation and after-care area outside Greater London, would be payable by virtue of that paragraph by the local authority.

Provision of accommodation by local authorities for the probation and after-care service

17.—(1) In any case in which a local authority would be liable under paragraph 15(1) or (3) above to defray all or part of the expenses incurred by a probation and after-care committee in providing any accommodation, the local authority may, subject to the provisions of this paragraph, itself provide the accommodation in question for the use of the committee.

(2) A local authority shall not by virtue of this paragraph provide any accommodation for the use of a probation and after-care committee except with the agreement—

(*a*) of the committee ; and

(*b*) if the expenses of the committee in providing the accommodation would have fallen to be defrayed partly by that authority and partly by one or more other local authorities, of the other local authority or authorities.

(3) Where in accordance with sub-paragraph (2)(*b*) above a local authority provides accommodation with the agreement of one or more other local authorities, that authority shall be entitled to

receive from the other authority or authorities such contribution to its expenditure in providing the accommodation as may be agreed between them or as in default of agreement may be determined by the Secretary of State. SCH. 3

Rules

18.—(1) The Secretary of State may make rules—

(*a*) regulating the constitution, procedure, powers and duties of probation and after-care committees, community service committees and case committees, and the expenses which may be incurred by them and the manner in which those expenses are to be defrayed ;

(*b*) regulating the qualifications, manner of appointment, conditions of service and duties of probation officers and staff appointed under paragraph 10 above ;

(*c*) prescribing anything else which under the preceding provisions of this Schedule may be prescribed ;

and in those provisions the expression "prescribed" means prescribed by rules of the Secretary of State.

(2) Without prejudice to sub-paragraph (1) above, the Secretary of State may by rules made under this Schedule make provision as to the manner in which paragraph 13 above is to be administered, and in particular may make provision—

(*a*) for prescribing the rates of allowances and the forms to be used and the particulars to be provided for the purpose of claiming payment of the allowances under that paragraph ; and

(*b*) for avoiding duplication between payments under that paragraph and under other arrangements where expenditure is incurred for more than one purpose, and otherwise for preventing abuses.

(3) Nothing in any rules made under this paragraph with respect to the constitution, procedure and functions of case committees shall apply to a case committee for an area within the inner London area, except in so far as may be determined under paragraph 5(2) above by the probation and after-care committee for that area.

Interpretation

19.—(1) In this Schedule, "the inner London area" has the same meaning as in the Administration of Justice Act 1964. 1964 c. 42.

(2) Where a probation and after-care area constituted by an order under paragraph 1(1) above is co-extensive with, or includes, a metropolitan county, the local authority for the purposes of this Schedule shall, so far as relates to the area of the metropolitan county, be the county council alone (and not the councils of the metropolitan districts within that county).

Section 55.

SCHEDULE 4

Transitional Provisions

General

1. Without prejudice to the provisions of section 38 of the Interpretation Act 1889 (effect of repeals)— 1889 c. 63.

(*a*) nothing in any repeal made by this Act shall affect any order or rule made, certificate issued, requirement or condition imposed or thing done under any enactment repealed by this Act, and every such order, rule, certificate, requirement, condition or thing shall, if in force at the commencement of this Act, continue in force (subject to the provisions of this Act) and be deemed to have been made, issued, imposed or done under the corresponding provisions of this Act; and

(*b*) any reference in any document (including an enactment) to any enactment repealed by this Act, whether a specific reference or a reference to provisions of a description which includes, or apart from any repeal made by this Act includes, the enactment so repealed, shall be construed as a reference to the corresponding enactment in this Act.

Transitional provisions with respect to repeals made by the Children and Young Persons Act 1969

2.—(1) The modifications of sections 51 and 57 of this Act contained in sub-paragraphs (2) and (3) below shall have effect for the purpose of preserving certain words omitted from sections 77 and 80 of the Criminal Justice Act 1948 by repeals made by the Children and Young Persons Act 1969, in so far as the relevant repeals are not yet in force at the commencement of this Act; and an order may be made by the Secretary of State under section 73(2) and (3) of the Children and Young Persons Act 1969 with respect to any such modification as if providing that any such modification shall cease to have effect constituted bringing the repeal of the words preserved by the modification into force, and as if that repeal and any of the following provisions of this paragraph were a provision of that Act. 1948 c. 58. 1969 c. 54.

(2) In section 51 of this Act—

(*a*) in subsection (1)(*a*), after the word " homes " where it first occurs there shall be inserted the words " or in remand homes or approved schools " and for the words " officers or servants in such hostels or homes " there shall be substituted the words " such officers or servants as aforesaid "; and

(*b*) in subsection (4)(*c*), after the word " serving " there shall be inserted the words " in remand homes or " and after the word " homes " there shall be inserted the words " or in approved schools ".

(3) In section 57 of this Act the following definitions shall be inserted at the appropriate points in alphabetical order:—

" ' approved school ' means a school approved under section 79 of the Children and Young Persons Act 1933;

'remand home' means premises established or used by the council of a county or county borough under the provisions of section 77 of the Children and Young Persons Act 1933". SCH. 4

SCHEDULE 5

Section 56(1).

CONSEQUENTIAL AMENDMENTS

The Children and Young Persons Act 1933

1933 c. 12.

1. In section 55 of the Children and Young Persons Act 1933 (power to order parent to pay fine etc. instead of child or young person), in subsection (1), for the words "section 1 of the Criminal Justice Act 1972" there shall be substituted the words "section 35 of the Powers of Criminal Courts Act 1973".

The Criminal Justice Act 1948

1948 c. 58.

2. In section 19 of the Criminal Justice Act 1948 (orders requiring attendance at an attendance centre), in subsection (1), for the words "section six of this Act" there shall be substituted the words "section six of the Powers of Criminal Courts Act 1973".

The Criminal Justice (Scotland) Act 1949

1949 c. 94.

3. In section 7 of the Criminal Justice (Scotland) Act 1949 (probation orders relating to persons residing in England)—

(*a*) in subsection (1), for the words "petty sessional division" and "that division" there shall be substituted respectively the words "petty sessions area" and "that area";

(*b*) in subsection (4), for the words from "the Criminal Justice Act 1948" to the end of the subsection there shall be substituted the words "the Powers of Criminal Courts Act 1973 (except section 8 of that Act) shall apply to the order as if it were a probation order made under section 2 of that Act:

Provided that section 6(2)(a), (3)(d) and (6) of that Act shall not apply to any such order and section 6(4) and (5) of that Act shall have effect respectively in relation to any such order as if for the first reference in section 6(4) to the Crown Court there were substituted a reference to a court in Scotland and as if for the second such reference therein and for both such references in section 6(5) there were substituted references to the court in Scotland by which the probation order was made or amended under this section";

(*c*) in subsection (5), for the words from "petty sessional division" to "1948)" there shall be substituted the words "petty sessions area for which the supervising court within the meaning of the Powers of Criminal Courts Act 1973";

Sch. 5

(*d*) in subsection (6), for the words " court of summary jurisdiction " in both places where they occur there shall be substituted the words " magistrates' court " ;

(*e*) in subsection (7), for the words " petty sessional division " in both places where they occur there shall be substituted the words " petty sessions area " ;

(*f*) in subsection (8), for the words " section nine of the Criminal Justice Act 1948 " there shall be substituted the words " section 10 of the Powers of Criminal Courts Act 1973 " and for the words " section three " there shall be substituted the words " section 2 ".

1952 c. 55.

The Magistrates' Courts Act 1952

4. In section 29 of the Magistrates' Courts Act 1952 (committal for sentence for indictable offence tried summarily), for the words " section twenty-nine of the Criminal Justice Act 1948 " there shall be substituted the words " section 42 of the Powers of Criminal Courts Act 1973 ".

5. In section 64 of that Act (enforcement of sums adjudged to be paid) in subsection (1), after the words " seven of this Act " there shall be inserted the words " and section nineteen of the Powers of Criminal Courts Act 1973 ".

6. In section 72B of that Act (transfer of fine orders from Scotland), in subsection (3), for the words " section 44(3) of the Criminal Justice Act 1967 " there shall be substituted the words " section 32(1) of the Powers of Criminal Courts Act 1973 ".

7. In section 110(1) of that Act (detention of offenders for one day in court-house or police station) the words " thirty-nine or " (inserted by the Criminal Justice Act 1967) shall cease to have effect.

1967 c. 80.

1954 c. 48.

The Summary Jurisdiction (Scotland) Act 1954

8. In section 44 of the Summary Jurisdiction (Scotland) Act 1954 (transfer of fine orders within and from Scotland), in subsection (5), for the words " section 47 of the Criminal Justice Act 1967 " there shall be substituted the words " section 31 of the Powers of Criminal Courts Act 1973 ".

1957 c. 27.

The Solicitors Act 1957

9. In section 38 of the Solicitors Act 1957 (control of employment of certain clerks), in subsection (5)(*a*), for the words " Criminal Justice Act 1948 " and " section twelve of that Act " there shall be substituted respectively the words " Powers of Criminal Courts Act 1973 " and " section 13 of that Act ".

SCH. 5

The Metropolitan Magistrates' Courts Act 1959

10. In section 3 of the Metropolitan Magistrates' Courts Act 1959 (power of Receiver for the Metropolitan Police District to provide premises for probation purposes), in subsection (2), for the words " section seventy-seven of the Criminal Justice Act 1948 " there shall be substituted the words " section 51 of the Powers of Criminal Courts Act 1973 ", and for the words " Fifth Schedule " in both places where they occur there shall be substituted the words " Third Schedule ". 1959 c. 45.

The First Offenders (Scotland) Act 1960

1960 c. 23.

11. In section 1 of the First Offenders (Scotland) Act 1960 (restriction on imprisonment of first offenders), in subsection (3A), for the words in paragraph (*b*) " section 12 of the Criminal Justice Act 1948 " there shall be substituted the words " section 13 of the Powers of Criminal Courts Act 1973 ".

The Criminal Justice Act 1961

1961 c. 39.

12. In section 5(5) of the Criminal Justice Act 1961 (construction of references to terms of imprisonment), for the words " sections fourteen and fifteen of the Criminal Justice Act 1948 " there shall be substituted the words " sections 31 and 32 of the Powers of Criminal Courts Act 1973 ".

13. In section 39(1) of that Act (interpretation), in the definition of " the statutory restrictions upon the imprisonment of young offenders ", for the words from " subsection (1) " to " 1952 " there shall be substituted the words " section 19(1) of the Powers of Criminal Courts Act 1973 ".

The Administration of Justice Act 1964

1964 c. 42.

14. In section 37 of the Administration of Justice Act 1964 (financial provisions), in subsection (4), for the words " section 77(3)(*a*) of the Criminal Justice Act 1948 " there shall be substituted the words " section 51(3)(*a*) of the Powers of Criminal Courts Act 1973 ", and the following shall be substituted for paragraph (*b*)—

" (*b*) in relation to payments under section 51(3)(*a*) of the said Act of 1973, expenses under Schedule 3 to that Act ; ".

The Fugitive Offenders Act 1967

1967 c. 68.

15. In section 15 of the Fugitive Offenders Act 1967 (restoration of persons not tried or acquitted or discharged), in subsection (2)(*b*), for the words " the Criminal Justice Act 1948 " there shall be substituted the words " the Powers of Criminal Courts Act 1973 ".

SCH. 5

The Criminal Justice Act 1967

1967 c. 80. 16. In section 26 of the Criminal Justice Act 1967 (restrictions on passing sentence in the absence of the defendant), in subsection (1), for the words "section 40 of this Act" there shall be substituted the words "section 23 of the Powers of Criminal Courts Act 1973".

17. In section 32 of that Act (amendments of Costs in Criminal Cases Act 1952), in subsection (3)(*a*), for the words "section 4 of the Criminal Justice Act 1948" there shall be substituted the words "section 3 of the Powers of Criminal Courts Act 1973".

18. In section 48 of that Act (enforcement in Scotland of fines imposed by the Crown Court), in subsection (1), for the words "the last foregoing section" there shall be substituted the words "section 31 of the Powers of Criminal Courts Act 1973".

19. In section 54 of that Act (miscellaneous provisions as to probation orders), in subsection (8)—

(*a*) in paragraph (*a*), for the words "section 4(2) of the Criminal Justice Act 1948" there shall be substituted the words "section 3(2) of the Powers of Criminal Courts Act 1973", and for the words "the said sections 3 and 4" there shall be substituted the words "section 3 of the said Act of 1949 and section 3 of the said Act of 1973";

(*b*) in paragraph (*b*), for the words "the said section 4" in the first place where they occur there shall be substituted the words "section 3 of the said Act of 1973" and for those words in the second place where they occur there shall be substituted the words "that section".

20. In section 56 of that Act (committal for sentence for offences tried summarily)—

(*a*) in subsection (1)(*a*), for the words "section 41(1) of this Act" there shall be substituted the words "section 24(1) of the Powers of Criminal Courts Act 1973"; and

(*b*) in subsection (2), for the words from "section 8(4)" to the end there shall be substituted the words "sections 28 and 29 of the Magistrates' Courts Act 1952 (committal for sentence), section 62(6) of this Act and sections 8(6) (probationer convicted of subsequent offence) and 24(2) (committal to be dealt with in respect of a suspended sentence) of the Powers of Criminal Courts Act 1973".

21. In section 62 of that Act (revocation of licences and conviction of prisoners on licence), in subsection (6), for the words "section 29 of the Criminal Justice Act 1948" there shall be substituted the words "section 42 of the Powers of Criminal Courts Act 1973".

22. In section 67 of that Act (computation of sentences of imprisonment passed in England and Wales), in subsection (2), for the words "section 40 of this Act" there shall be substituted the words "section 23 of the Powers of Criminal Courts Act 1973".

23. In section 73 of that Act (power to order legal aid to be given), there shall be inserted after subsection (8) (in place of the subsection inserted by Schedule 5 to the Criminal Justice Act 1972) the following subsection— SCH. 5

"(8A) Where a person makes an application to a magistrates' court under section 37 of the Powers of Criminal Courts Act 1973 (review of compensation orders) the court may order that he shall be given legal aid for the purpose of the proceedings before the court ".

24. In section 74 of that Act (supplementary provisions as to legal aid orders), in subsection (12), for the words from " or 8 " to " this Act " there shall be substituted the words " 8, 16, 17(1) or (2), 23 or 27 of the Powers of Criminal Courts Act 1973 ".

25. In section 84(1) of that Act (interpretation of Part IV of that Act), in the definition of " committed for sentence " for the words from " section 6 " to " this Act " there shall be substituted the words " section 28 or 29 of the Magistrates' Courts Act 1952, section 67 of the Mental Health Act 1959, section 62(6) of the Criminal Justice Act 1967, or section 6, 8, 16, 17(2)(*b*) or 24 of the Powers of Criminal Courts Act 1973 ".

26. In section 104 of that Act (general provisions as to interpretation), in subsection (1)—

(*a*) for the definition of " extended sentence certificate " there shall be substituted the following—

" ' extended sentence certificate ' means a certificate issued under section 28 of the Powers of Criminal Courts Act 1973 stating that an extended term of imprisonment was imposed on an offender under that section " ; and

(*b*) for the definition of " suspended sentence " there shall be substituted the following—

" ' suspended sentence ' means a sentence to which an order under section 22(1) of the Powers of Criminal Courts Act 1973 relates ".

27. In section 106(2)(*b*) of that Act (provisions extending to Scotland), for the words from " 38(7) " to " 54(6) to " there shall be substituted the words " 48, 54(6) and ".

Criminal Appeal Act 1968 1968 c. 19.

28. In section 10 of the Criminal Appeal Act 1968 (appeal against sentence in cases dealt with by the Crown Court otherwise than on conviction on indictment), in subsection (3)(*c*)(iii), for the words " section 40 of the Criminal Justice Act 1967 " there shall be substituted the words " section 23 of the Powers of Criminal Courts Act 1973 ".

29. In section 11 of that Act (supplementary provisions as to appeal against sentence), in subsection (4)—

(*a*) for the words " section 40(1) of the Criminal Justice Act 1967 " there shall be substituted the words " section 23(1) of the Powers of Criminal Courts Act 1973 " ; and

(*b*) for the words in paragraph (*b*) " the said section 40(1) " there shall be substituted the words " the said section 23(1) ".

Sch. 5

The Social Work (Scotland) Act 1968

1968 c. 49.

30. In section 94 of the Social Work (Scotland) Act 1968 (interpretation), in subsection (1), in the definition of " probation order " for the words " section 3 of the Criminal Justice Act 1948 " there shall be substituted the words " section 2 of the Powers of Criminal Courts Act 1973 ".

The Civil Evidence Act 1968

1968 c. 64.

31. In section 11 of the Civil Evidence Act 1968 (convictions as evidence in civil proceedings), in subsection (5), for the words in paragraph (*a*) " section 12 of the Criminal Justice Act 1948 " there shall be substituted the words " section 13 of the Powers of Criminal Courts Act 1973 ".

The Law Reform (Miscellaneous Provisions) (Scotland) Act 1968

1968 c. 70.

32. In section 10 of the Law Reform (Miscellaneous Provisions) (Scotland) Act 1968 (convictions as evidence in civil proceedings), in subsection (5), for the words in paragraph (*a*) " section 12 of the Criminal Justice Act 1948 " there shall be substituted the words " section 13 of the Powers of Criminal Courts Act 1973 ".

The Children and Young Persons Act 1969

1969 c. 54.

33. In section 3(6) of the Children and Young Persons Act 1969 (powers of court where it finds offence condition satisfied in care proceedings), in paragraph (*a*), for the words " section 1 of the Criminal Justice Act 1972 " there shall be substituted the words " section 35 of the Powers of Criminal Courts Act 1973 ".

34. In section 6 of that Act (summary trial of young persons), in subsection (3), for the words " section 107(2) of the said Act of 1952 " there shall be substituted the words " section 19(1) of the Powers of Criminal Courts Act 1973 ".

35. In section 13 of that Act (selection of supervisor for person subject to a supervision order), in subsection (2), for the words from " by paragraph " to " paragraph 6(*b*) " there shall be substituted the words " on probation officers by paragraph 8 of Schedule 3 to the Powers of Criminal Courts Act 1973 or by rules under paragraph 18(1)(*b*) ".

36. In section 46 of that Act (discontinuance of approved schools, etc., on establishment of community homes), in subsection (1), for the words from " remand home " to " 1948 " there shall be substituted the words " or remand home within the meaning of the Criminal Justice Act 1948 or approved probation hostel or approved probation home within the meaning of the Powers of Criminal Courts Act 1973 ".

SCH. 5

37. In section 48 of that Act (financial provisions applicable on cessation of controlled or assisted community home), in subsection (5)(*b*), for the words " section 77(3)(*b*) of the Criminal Justice Act 1948 " there shall be substituted the words " section 51(3)(*c*) of the Powers of Criminal Courts Act 1973 ".

38. In Schedule 3 to that Act (provisions as to approved schools and other institutions)—

(*a*) in paragraphs 6(1) and 9(2)(*b*), for the words " section 77 of the Criminal Justice Act 1948 " there shall be substituted the words " section 51 of the Powers of Criminal Courts Act 1973 " ;

(*b*) in paragraph 9(4)(*b*), for the words " Schedule 5 to the Criminal Justice Act 1948 " there shall be substituted the words " Schedule 3 to the Powers of Criminal Courts Act 1973 " ;

(*c*) in paragraph 10(4)(*b*), after the words " section 77(3)(*b*) of the Criminal Justice Act 1948 " there shall be inserted the words " or under section 51(3)(*c*) of the Powers of Criminal Courts Act 1973 ".

39. In Schedule 4 to that Act (transitional provisions and savings) in paragraph 12(3), for the words " Criminal Justice Act 1948 " there shall be substituted the words " Powers of Criminal Courts Act 1973 ".

The Administration of Justice Act 1970

1970 c. 31.

40. In Part I of Schedule 9 to the Administration of Justice Act 1970 (orders for costs, compensation, etc., enforceable as on a summary conviction), for paragraphs 10 and 11 as originally enacted there shall be substituted (in place of the paragraph substituted for those paragraphs and the paragraph 9A inserted by section 8 of the Criminal Damage Act 1971 by Schedule 5 to the Criminal Justice Act 1972) the following paragraph—

" 10. Where under section 35 of the Powers of Criminal Courts Act 1973 a court orders the payment of compensation.".

The Courts Act 1971

1971 c. 23.

41. In section 53 of the Courts Act 1971 (administrative functions of justices), in subsection (7)(*a*), for the words " made under paragraph 1 of Schedule 5 to the Criminal Justice Act 1948 " there shall be substituted the words " deemed to be made under paragraph 1 of Schedule 3 to the Powers of Criminal Courts Act 1973 ".

The Industrial Relations Act 1971

1971 c. 72.

42. In paragraph 28 of Schedule 3 to the Industrial Relations Act 1971 (provisions as to fines imposed by the Industrial Court), in subparagraph (1), for the words from " section 14 " to " 1967 " there shall be substituted the words " the provisions of sections 31 and 32 of the Powers of Criminal Courts Act 1973 " and the words " to a court of assize or " shall be omitted.

SCH. 5

The Road Traffic Act 1972

1972 c. 20.

43. In section 102 of the Road Traffic Act 1972 (combination of disqualification and endorsement with probation orders and orders for discharge in England and Wales), for the words, in subsection (1), " section 12(2) of the Criminal Justice Act 1948 ", and for the words, in subsection (2), " section 12(1) of the said Act of 1948 ", there shall be substituted respectively the words " section 13(3) of the Powers of Criminal Courts Act 1973 " and " section 13(1) of the said Act of 1973 ".

44. In section 105 of that Act (supplementary provisions as to disqualifications and endorsements), in subsection (2), after the words " Criminal Justice Act 1972 " there shall be inserted the words " or section 44(3) of the Powers of Criminal Courts Act 1973 " and for the words " that section " there shall be substituted the words " section 24 or 44, as the case may be ".

1972 c. 71.

The Criminal Justice Act 1972

45. In section 23 of the Criminal Justice Act 1972 (power to deprive offender of property used, or intended for use, for purposes of crime), in subsection (5), for the words from " in regard " to " of this section " there shall be substituted the words " that any property which was in his possession or under his control at the time of his apprehension—

(*a*) has been used for the purpose of committing, or facilitating the commission of, any offence ; or

(*b*) was intended by him to be used for that purpose ".

46. In section 24 of that Act (driving disqualification where vehicle used for purposes of crime)—

(*a*) in subsection (2), for the words from " mentioned " to the end of the subsection there shall be substituted the words " of committing, or facilitating the commission of, the offence, the court may order that person to be disqualified, for such period as the court thinks fit, for holding or obtaining a licence to drive a motor vehicle granted under Part III of the Road Traffic Act 1972 " ; and

(*b*) in subsection (3), for the words " subsection (1) " there shall be substituted the words " subsection (2) ".

47. In section 49 of that Act (community service order in lieu of warrant of commitment for failure to pay fine, etc.)—

(*a*) in subsection (2), for the words from the beginning to " this Act " in the second place where it occurs there shall be substituted the words " In this section ' community service order ' has the same meaning as in the Powers of Criminal Courts Act 1973 and section 14(2) of that Act and, so far as applicable, the other provisions of that Act ", and for the words " subsection (3) of section 17 " and " section 18(1)(*b*) of this Act " there shall be substituted respectively the words " subsection (3) of section 16 " and " section 17(2)(*a*) of that Act " ; and

Sch. 5

(*b*) in subsection (4), for the words " section 47(3) of the Criminal Justice Act 1967 " there shall be substituted the words " section 32(1) of the Powers of Criminal Courts Act 1973 ".

48. In Schedule 2 to that Act (ineligibility and disqualification for and excusal from jury service), in the entry relating to probation homes and hostels and bail hostels, for the words " (as defined in section 53 of this Act) " there shall be substituted the words " (within the meaning of the Powers of Criminal Courts Act 1973) ".

The Costs in Criminal Cases Act 1973

1973 c. 14.

49. In section 18 of the Costs in Criminal Cases Act 1973 (miscellaneous applications of that Act)—

(*a*) in subsection (1)(*b*), for the words " section 29 of that Act " there shall be substituted the words " section 42 of the Powers of Criminal Courts Act 1973 " ; and

(*b*) in subsection (4), for paragraphs (*a*), (*b*) and (*c*) there shall be substituted the following paragraphs—

" (*a*) proceedings for dealing with an offender under section 6, 8 or 10 of the Powers of Criminal Courts Act 1973 (probation orders and orders for conditional discharge) ;

(*b*) proceedings under section 16 or 17 of that Act (community service orders) ; and

(*c*) proceedings under section 23(1) or 27 of that Act for dealing with an offender in respect of a suspended sentence or for breach of a suspended sentence supervision order ".

The Social Security Act 1973

1973 c. 38.

50. In Schedule 23 to the Social Security Act 1973 (proceedings for offences, etc.), in paragraph 11(1), for the words " Criminal Justice Act 1948 " there shall be substituted the words " Powers of Criminal Courts Act 1973 ".

Section 56(2).

SCHEDULE 6

ENACTMENTS REPEALED

Chapter	Short Title	Extent of Repeal
11 & 12 Geo. 6. c. 58.	The Criminal Justice Act 1948.	Sections 3 to 12 and 14. Section 17(1), (2) and (6). Sections 29, 43 and 45 to 47. Section 77, except subsection (6), and, in subsection (1), the words "Any expenses of the Secretary of State under this Act" and the words from "shall" to the end of the subsection. In section 80, in subsection (1) the definitions of "approved probation hostel", "approved probation home", "offence the sentence for which is fixed by law", "order for conditional discharge", "period of conditional discharge", "probationer", "probation order", "probation period", "sum adjudged to be paid by a conviction" and "supervising court", and subsection (5). Section 81, so far as relates to sections 8, 9, 11 and 12. Schedules 1 and 5. In Schedule 8, paragraphs 3 to 9.
12, 13 & 14 Geo. 6. c. 94.	The Criminal Justice (Scotland) Act 1949.	In Schedule 11, the entry relating to section 9 of the Criminal Justice Act 1948.
12, 13 & 14 Geo. 6. c. 101.	The Justices of the Peace Act 1949.	Sections 36 and 37.
15 & 16 Geo. 6 & 1 Eliz. 2. c. 55.	The Magistrates' Courts Act 1952.	Section 107(2), (3). In section 110(1), the words "thirty-nine or".
7 & 8 Eliz. 2. c. 72.	The Mental Health Act 1959.	In Part I of Schedule 7, the entry relating to the Criminal Justice Act 1948.
9 & 10 Eliz. 2. c. 39.	The Criminal Justice Act 1961.	Section 2(2). Section 9.
1964 c. 42.	The Administration of Justice Act 1964.	Section 22. In section 31, subsection (1) in so far as it amends s. 36 of the Justices of the Peace Act 1949. In Schedule 3, paragraph 19(2), (3).
1967 c. 58.	The Criminal Law Act 1967.	Section 7.
1967 c. 80.	The Criminal Justice Act 1967.	Sections 37 to 42. Section 47. In section 48, in subsection (1) the words "of a magistrates' court or", the words from

Sch. 6

Chapter	Short Title	Extent of Repeal
1967 c. 80 —*cont.*	The Criminal Justice Act 1967—*cont.*	" section 72A " to " Scotland) or ", and the words " magistrates' court or ", and subsection (2). In section 50, the words from " and in " to the end of the section. Sections 52 and 53. In section 54, subsections (1) to (3), (5) and (7). Sections 55 and 57. Section 95 except subsection (1). Section 96. Section 99. Section 106(3)(*b*), so far as relates to section 38(7). In Schedule 6, paragraph 6.
1968 c. 69.	The Justices of the Peace Act 1968.	Section 4(5) and (6).
1969 c. 54.	The Children and Young Persons Act 1969.	Section 7(2). In Schedule 4, paragraph 5(2). In Schedule 5, paragraph 45.
1971 c. 23.	The Courts Act 1971.	Section 53(2)(*a*). In Schedule 8:— in paragraph 24, sub-paragraph (*a*) and in sub-paragraph (*b*) the words " 14(5) "; paragraphs 25 to 27; paragraph 48(*a*), so far as relates to sections 40, 41, 47, 48 and 54 of the Criminal Justice Act 1967; paragraphs 51, 53 and 54.
1971 c. 72.	The Industrial Relations Act 1971.	In Schedule 3, in paragraph 28(1) the words " to a court of assize or ".
1972 c. 70.	The Local Government Act 1972.	In section 217(5), the words from " but " to the end of the subsection.
1972 c. 71.	The Criminal Justice Act 1972.	Part I except sections 6, 23(5) and (6), and 24(2) to (4). Sections 37, 40, 51(3), 52 to 57, and 66(3) and (4). Schedule 1. In Schedule 5, the entry relating to the Criminal Justice Act 1948, paragraphs (*b*), (*e*), (*f*) and (*g*) of the entry relating to the Criminal Justice Act 1967, and paragraph (*b*) of the entry relating to Part I of Schedule 9 to the Administration of Justice Act 1970.

PRODUCED IN ENGLAND BY COMMERCIAL COLOUR PRESS LONDON
FOR HAROLD GLOVER
Controller of Her Majesty's Stationery Office and Queens' Printer of Acts of Parliament
Dd.252489 K.56 7/75 CCP